Aesop's Fables 1

Aesop's Fables 1

Aesop | Arthur Rackham

THE CLASSIC

contents

1. Belling the Cat

The Mice once called a meeting to decide on a plan to free themselves of their enemy, the Cat. At least they wished to find some way of knowing when she was coming, so they might have time to run away.

Indeed, something had to be done, for they lived in such constant fear of her claws that they hardly dared stir from their dens by night or day. Many plans were discussed, but none of them was thought good enough. At last a very young Mouse got up and said:

"I have a plan that seems very simple, but I know it will be successful. All we have to do is to hang a bell about the Cat's neck.

When we hear the bell ringing we will know immediately that our enemy is coming."

All the Mice were much surprised that they had not thought of such a plan before. But in the midst of the rejoicing over their good fortune, an old Mouse arose and said:

"I will say that the plan of the young Mouse is very good. But let me ask one question: Who will bell the Cat?"

It is one thing to say that something should be done,
but quite a different matter to do it.

2. The Fox and the Grapes

A Fox one day spied a beautiful bunch of ripe grapes hanging from a vine trained along the branches of a tree. The grapes seemed ready to burst with juice, and the Fox's mouth watered as he gazed longingly at them. The bunch hung from a high branch, and the Fox had to jump for it. The first time he jumped he missed it by a long way.

So he walked off a short distance and took a running leap at it, only to fall short once more. Again and again he tried, but in vain.

Now he sat down and looked at the grapes in disgust.

"What a fool I am," he said. "Here I am wearing myself out to get a bunch of sour grapes that are not worth gaping for."

And off he walked very, very scornfully.

There are many who pretend to despise and belittle
that which is beyond their reach.

3. Jupiter and the Tortoise

Jupiter was about to marry a wife, and determined to celebrate the event by inviting all the animals to a banquet. They all came except the Tortoise, who did not put in an appearance, much to Jupiter's surprise. So when he next saw the Tortoise he asked him why he had not been at the banquet. "I don't care for going out," said the Tortoise; "there's no place like home."

Jupiter was so much annoyed by this reply that he decreed that from that time forth the Tortoise should carry his house upon his back, and never be able to get away from home even if he wished to.

People often prefer to live simply at home than to live lavishly at someone else's house.

4. The Tortoise and the Ducks

The Tortoise, you know, carries his house on his back. No matter how hard he tries, he cannot leave home. They say that Jupiter punished him so, because he was such a lazy stay-at-home that he would not go to Jupiter's wedding, even when especially invited.

After many years, Tortoise began to wish he had gone to that wedding. When he saw how gaily the birds flew about and how the Hare and the Chipmunk and all the other animals ran nimbly by, always eager to see everything there was to be seen, the Tortoise felt very sad and discontented. He wanted to see the world too, and there he was with a house on his back and little short legs that could hardly drag him along.

One day he met a pair of Ducks and told them all his trouble.

"We can help you to see the world," said the Ducks. "Take hold of this stick with your teeth and we will carry you far up in the air where you can see the whole countryside. But keep quiet or you will be sorry."

The Tortoise was very glad indeed. He seized the stick firmly with his teeth, the two Ducks took hold of it one at each end, and away they sailed up toward the clouds.

Just then a Crow flew by. He was very much astonished at the strange sight and cried:

"This must surely be the King of Tortoises!"

"Why certainly—" began the Tortoise.

But as he opened his mouth to say these foolish words he lost his hold on the stick, and down he fell to the ground, where he was dashed to pieces on a rock.

Foolish curiosity and vanity often lead to misfortune.

5. The Young Crab and His Mother

"Why in the world do you walk sideways like that?" said a Mother Crab to her son. "You should always walk straight forward with your toes turned out."

"Show me how to walk, mother dear," answered the little Crab obediently, "I want to learn."

So the old Crab tried and tried to walk straight forward. But she could walk sideways only, like her son. And when she wanted to turn her toes out she tripped and fell on her nose.

Do not tell others how to act
unless you can set a good example.

6. The Frogs and the Ox

An Ox came down to a reedy pool to drink. As he splashed heavily into the water, he crushed a young Frog into the mud. The old Frog soon missed the little one and asked his brothers and sisters what had become of him.

"A great big monster," said one of them, "stepped on little brother with one of his huge feet!"

"Big, was he!" said the old Frog, puffing herself up. "Was he as big as this?"

"Oh, much bigger!" they cried.

The Frog puffed up still more.

"He could not have been bigger than this," she said. But the little Frogs all declared that the monster was much, much big-

ger and the old Frog kept puffing herself out more and more until, all at once, she burst.

Do not attempt the impossible.

7. The Dog, the Cock, and the Fox

A Dog and a Cock, who were the best of friends, wished very much to see something of the world. So they decided to leave the farmyard and to set out into the world along the road that led to the woods. The two comrades traveled along in the very best of spirits and without meeting any adventure to speak of.

At nightfall the Cock, looking for a place to roost, as was his custom, spied near-by a hollow tree that he thought would do very nicely for a night's lodging. The Dog could creep inside and the Cock would fly up on one of the branches. So said, so done, and both slept very comfortably.

With the first glimmer of dawn the Cock

awoke. For the moment he forgot just where he was. He thought he was still in the farmyard where it had been his duty to arouse the household at daybreak. So standing on tip-toes he flapped his wings and crowed lustily. But instead of awakening the farmer, he awakened a Fox not far off in the wood. The Fox immediately had rosy visions of a very delicious breakfast. Hurrying to the tree where the Cock was roosting, he said very politely:

"A hearty welcome to our woods, honored sir. I cannot tell you how glad I am to see you here. I am quite sure we shall become the closest of friends."

"I feel highly flattered, kind sir," replied the Cock slyly. "If you will please go around to the door of my house at the foot of the tree, my porter will let you in."

The hungry but unsuspecting Fox, went around the tree as he was told, and in a twinkling the Dog had seized him.

Those who try to deceive may expect to be paid in their own coin.

8. The Eagle and the Jackdaw

An Eagle, swooping down on powerful wings, seized a lamb in her talons and made off with it to her nest. A Jackdaw saw the deed, and his silly head was filled with the idea that he was big and strong enough to do as the Eagle had done. So with much rustling of feathers and a fierce air, he came down swiftly on the back of a large Ram. But when he tried to rise again he found that he could not get away, for his claws were tangled in the wool. And so far was he from carrying away the Ram, that the Ram hardly noticed he was there.

The Shepherd saw the fluttering Jackdaw and at once guessed what had happened. Running up, he caught the bird and clipped its wings. That evening he gave the Jackdaw to his children.

"What a funny bird this is!" they said laughing, "what do you call it, father?"

"That is a Jackdaw, my children. But if you should ask him, he would say he is an Eagle."

Do not let your vanity make you overestimate your powers.

9. The Boy and the Filberts

A Boy was given permission to put his hand into a pitcher to get some filberts. But he took such a great fistful that he could not draw his hand out again. There he stood, unwilling to give up a single filbert and yet unable to get them all out at once. Vexed and disappointed he began to cry.

"My boy," said his mother, "be satisfied with half the nuts you have taken and you will easily get your hand out. Then perhaps you may have some more filberts some other time."

Do not attempt too much at once.

10. Hercules and the Wagoner

A Farmer was driving his wagon along a miry country road after a heavy rain. The horses could hardly drag the load through the deep mud, and at last came to a standstill when one of the wheels sank to the hub in a rut.

The farmer climbed down from his seat and stood beside the wagon looking at it but without making the least effort to get it out of the rut. All he did was to curse his bad luck and call loudly on Hercules to come to his aid. Then, it is said, Hercules really did appear, saying:

"Put your shoulder to the wheel, man, and urge on your horses. Do you think you can move the wagon by simply looking at it and whining about it? Hercules will not help unless you make some effort to help yourself."

And when the farmer put his shoulder to the wheel and urged on the horses, the wagon moved very readily, and soon the Farmer was riding along in great content and with a good lesson learned.

Heaven helps those who help themselves.

11. The Kid and the Wolf

A frisky young Kid had been left by the herdsman on the thatched roof of a sheep shelter to keep him out of harm's way. The Kid was browsing near the edge of the roof, when he spied a Wolf and began to jeer at him, making faces and abusing him to his heart's content.

"I hear you," said the Wolf, "and I haven't the least grudge against you for what you say or do. When you are up there it is the roof that's talking, not you."

Do not say anything at any time that you would not say at all times.

12. The Town Mouse and the Country Mouse

A Town Mouse once visited a relative who lived in the country. For lunch the Country Mouse served wheat stalks, roots, and acorns, with a dash of cold water for drink. The Town Mouse ate very sparingly, nibbling a little of this and a little of that, and by her manner making it very plain that she ate the simple food only to be polite.

After the meal the friends had a long talk, or rather the Town Mouse talked about her life in the city while the Country Mouse listened. They then went to bed in a cozy nest in the hedgerow and slept in quiet and comfort until morning. In her sleep the Country Mouse dreamed she was a Town Mouse with all the luxuries and delights of city life that her friend had described for her. So the next day when the Town Mouse asked the Country Mouse to go home with her to the city, she gladly said yes.

When they reached the mansion in which the Town Mouse lived, they found on the table in the dining room the leavings of a very fine banquet. There were sweetmeats and jellies, pastries, delicious cheeses, indeed, the most tempting foods that a Mouse can imagine.

But just as the Country Mouse was about to nibble a dainty bit of pastry, she heard a Cat mew loudly and scratch at the door. In great fear the Mice scurried to a hiding place, where they lay quite still for a long time, hardly daring to breathe. When at last they ventured back to the feast, the door opened suddenly and in came the servants to clear the table, followed by the House Dog.

The Country Mouse stopped in the Town Mouse's den only long enough to pick up her carpet bag and umbrella.

"You may have luxuries and dainties that I have not," she said as she hurried away, "but I prefer my plain food and simple life in the country with the peace and security that go with it."

Poverty with security is better than plenty in the midst of fear and uncertainty.

13. The Stag and the Vine

A Stag, pursued by the huntsmen, concealed himself under cover of a thick Vine. They lost track of him and passed by his hiding-place without being aware that he was anywhere near. Supposing all danger to be over, he presently began to browse on the leaves of the Vine.

The movement drew the attention of the returning huntsmen, and one of them, supposing some animal to be hidden there, shot an arrow at a venture into the foliage. The unlucky Stag was pierced to the heart, and, as he expired, he said, "I deserve my fate for my treachery in feeding upon the leaves of my protector."

Ingratitude sometimes brings its own punishment.

14. The Ass and His Driver

An Ass was being driven along a road leading down the mountain side, when he suddenly took it into his silly head to choose his own path. He could see his stall at the foot of the mountain, and to him the quickest way down seemed to be over the edge of the nearest cliff. Just as he was about to leap over, his master caught him by the tail and tried to pull him back, but the stubborn Ass would not yield and pulled with all his might.

"Very well," said his master, "go your way, you willful beast, and see where it leads you."

With that he let go, and the foolish Ass tumbled head over heels down the mountain side.

They who will not listen to reason but stubbornly go their own way against the friendly advice of those who are wiser than they, are on the road to misfortune.

15. The Oxen and the Wheels

A pair of Oxen were drawing a heavily loaded wagon along a miry country road. They had to use all their strength to pull the wagon, but they did not complain.

The Wheels of the wagon were of a different sort. Though the task they had to do was very light compared with that of the Oxen, they creaked and groaned at every turn. The poor Oxen, pulling with all their might to draw the wagon through the deep mud, had their ears filled with the loud complaining of the Wheels. And this, you may well know, made their work so much the harder to endure.

"Silence!" the Oxen cried at last, out of patience. "What have you Wheels to complain about so loudly? We are drawing all the weight, not you, and we are keeping still about it besides."

They complain most who suffer least.

16. The Lion and the Mouse

A Lion lay asleep in the forest, his great head resting on his paws. A timid little Mouse came upon him unexpectedly, and in her fright and haste to get away, ran across the Lion's nose. Roused from his nap, the Lion laid his huge paw angrily on the tiny creature to kill her.

"Spare me!" begged the poor Mouse. "Please let me go and some day I will surely repay you."

The Lion was much amused to think that a Mouse could ever help him. But he was generous and finally let the Mouse go.

Some days later, while stalking his prey in the forest, the Lion was caught in the toils of a hunter's net. Unable to free himself, he filled the forest with his angry roaring.

The Mouse knew the voice and quickly found the Lion struggling in the net. Running to one of the great ropes that bound him, she gnawed it until it parted, and soon the Lion was free.

"You laughed when I said I would repay you," said the Mouse. "Now you see that even a Mouse can help a Lion."

A kindness is never wasted.

17. The Plane Tree

Two Travellers, walking in the noonday sun, sought the shade of a widespreading tree to rest. As they lay looking up among the pleasant leaves, they saw that it was a Plane Tree.

"How useless is the Plane!" said one of them. "It bears no fruit whatever, and only serves to litter the ground with leaves."

"Ungrateful creatures!" said a voice from the Plane Tree. "You lie here in my cooling shade, and yet you say I am useless! Thus ungratefully, O Jupiter, do men receive their blessings!"

Our best blessings are often the least appreciated.

18. The Shepherd Boy and the Wolf

A Shepherd Boy tended his master's Sheep near a dark forest not far from the village. Soon he found life in the pasture very dull. All he could do to amuse himself was to talk to his dog or play on his shepherd's pipe.

One day as he sat watching the Sheep and the quiet forest, and thinking what he would do should he see a Wolf, he thought of a plan to amuse himself. His Master had told him to call for help should a Wolf attack the flock, and the Villagers would drive it away. So now, though he had not seen anything that even looked like a Wolf, he ran toward the village shouting at the top of his voice, "Wolf! Wolf!"

As he expected, the Villagers who heard the cry dropped their work and ran in great excitement to the pasture. But when they got there they found the Boy doubled up with laughter at the trick he had played on them.

A few days later the Shepherd Boy again shouted, "Wolf! Wolf!" Again the Villagers ran to help him, only to be laughed at again.

Then one evening as the sun was setting behind the forest and the shadows were creeping out over the pasture, a Wolf really did spring from the underbrush and fall upon the Sheep.

In terror the Boy ran toward the village shouting "Wolf! Wolf!" But though the Villagers heard the cry, they did not run to help him as they had before. "He cannot fool us again," they said.

The Wolf killed a great many of the Boy's sheep and then slipped away into the forest.

Liars are not believed even when they speak the truth.

19. The Wolf and the Crane

A Wolf had been feasting too greedily, and a bone had stuck crosswise in his throat. He could get it neither up nor down, and of course he could not eat a thing. Naturally that was an awful state of affairs for a greedy Wolf. So away he hurried to the Crane. He was sure that she, with her long neck and bill, would easily be able to reach the bone and pull it out.

"I will reward you very handsomely," said the Wolf, "if you pull that bone out for me."

The Crane, as you can imagine, was very uneasy about putting her head in a Wolf's throat. But she was grasping in nature, so she did what the Wolf asked her to do. When the

Wolf felt that the bone was gone, he started to walk away.

"But what about my reward!" called the Crane anxiously.

"What!" snarled the Wolf, whirling around. "Haven't you got it? Isn't it enough that I let you take your head out of my mouth without snapping it off?"

Expect no reward for serving the wicked.

20. The Farmer and the Stork

A Stork of a very simple and trusting nature had been asked by a gay party of Cranes to visit a field that had been newly planted. But the party ended dismally with all the birds entangled in the meshes of the Farmer's net.

The Stork begged the Farmer to spare him.

"Please let me go," he pleaded. "I belong to the Stork family who you know are honest and birds of good character. Besides, I did not know the Cranes were going to steal."

"You may be a very good bird," answered the Farmer, "but I caught you with the thieving Cranes and you will have to share the same punishment with them."

You are judged by the company you keep.

21. The Sheep and the Pig

One day a shepherd discovered a fat Pig in the meadow where his Sheep were pastured. He very quickly captured the porker, which squealed at the top of its voice the moment the Shepherd laid his hands on it. You would have thought, to hear the loud squealing, that the Pig was being cruelly hurt. But in spite of its squeals and struggles to escape, the Shepherd tucked his prize under his arm and started off to the butcher's in the market place.

The Sheep in the pasture were much astonished and amused at the Pig's behavior, and followed the Shepherd and his charge to the pasture gate.

"What makes you squeal like that?"

asked one of the Sheep. “The Shepherd often catches and carries off one of us. But we should feel very much ashamed to make such a terrible fuss about it like you do.”

“That is all very well,” replied the Pig, with a squeal and a frantic kick. “When he catches you he is only after your wool. But he wants my bacon! Gree-ee-ee!”

It is easy to be brave when there is no danger.

22. The Travelers and the Purse

Two men were traveling in company along the road when one of them picked up a well-filled purse.

"How lucky I am!" he said. "I have found a purse. Judging by its weight it must be full of gold."

"Do not say 'I have found a purse,'" said his companion. "Say rather 'we have found a purse' and 'how lucky we are.' Travelers ought to share alike the fortunes or misfortunes of the road."

"No, no," replied the other angrily. "I found it and I am going to keep it."

Just then they heard a shout of "Stop, thief!" and looking around, saw a mob of people armed with clubs coming down the road.

The man who had found the purse fell into a panic.

"We are lost if they find the purse on us," he cried.

"No, no," replied the other, "You would not say 'we' before, so now stick to your 'I'. Say 'I am lost.'"

We cannot expect any one to share our misfortunes
unless we are willing to share our good fortune also.

23. The Lion and the Ass

One day as the Lion walked proudly down a forest aisle, and the animals respectfully made way for him, an Ass brayed a scornful remark as he passed. The Lion felt a flash of anger. But when he turned his head and saw who had spoken, he walked quietly on. He would not honor the fool with even so much as a stroke of his claws.

Do not resent the remarks of a fool. Ignore them.

24. The Gnat and the Bull

A Gnat flew over the meadow with much buzzing for so small a creature and settled on the tip of one of the horns of a Bull. After he had rested a short time, he made ready to fly away. But before he left he begged the Bull's pardon for having used his horn for a resting place.

"You must be very glad to have me go now," he said.

"It's all the same to me," replied the Bull. "I did not even know you were there."

We are often of greater importance in our own eyes than in the eyes of our neighbor.

The smaller the mind the greater the conceit.

25. The Owl and the Grasshopper

The Owl always takes her sleep during the day. Then after sundown, when the rosy light fades from the sky and the shadows rise slowly through the wood, out she comes ruffling and blinking from the old hollow tree. Now her weird "hoo-hoo-hoo-oo-oo" echoes through the quiet wood, and she begins her hunt for the bugs and beetles, frogs and mice she likes so well to eat.

Now there was a certain old Owl who had become very cross and hard to please as she grew older, especially if anything disturbed her daily slumbers. One warm summer afternoon as she dozed away in her den in the old oak tree, a Grasshopper nearby began a joyous but very raspy song. Out popped the old Owl's head from the opening in the tree that served her both for door and for window.

"Get away from here, sir," she said to the Grasshopper. "Have you no manners? You should at least respect my age and leave me to sleep in quiet!"

But the Grasshopper answered saucily that he had as much right to his place in the sun as the Owl had to her place in the old oak. Then he struck up a louder and still more rasping tune.

The wise old Owl knew quite well that it would do no good to argue with the Grasshopper, nor with anybody else for that matter. Besides, her eyes were not sharp enough by day to permit her to punish the Grasshopper as he deserved. So she laid aside all hard words and spoke very kindly to him.

"Well sir," she said, "if I must stay awake, I am going to settle right down to enjoy your singing. Now that I think of it, I have a wonderful wine here, sent me from Olympus, of which I am told Apollo drinks before he sings to the high gods. Please come up and taste this delicious drink with me. I know it will make you sing like Apollo himself."

The foolish Grasshopper was taken in by the Owl's flattering words. Up he jumped to the Owl's den, but as soon as he was near enough so the old Owl could see him clearly, she pounced upon him and ate him up.

Flattery is not a proof of true admiration. Do not let flattery throw you off your guard against an enemy.

26. The Rat and the Elephant

A Rat was traveling along the King's highway. He was a very proud Rat, considering his small size and the bad reputation all Rats have. As Mr. Rat walked along—he kept mostly to the ditch—he noticed a great commotion up the road, and soon a grand procession came in view. It was the King and his retinue.

The King rode on a huge Elephant adorned with the most gorgeous trappings. With the King in his luxurious howdah were the royal Dog and Cat. A great crowd of people followed the procession. They were so taken up with admiration of the Elephant, that the Rat was not noticed. His pride was hurt.

“What fools!” he cried. “Look at me, and you will soon forget that clumsy Elephant! Is it his great size that makes your eyes pop out? Or is it his wrinkled hide? Why, I have eyes and ears and as many legs as he! I am of just as much importance, and—”

But just then the royal Cat spied him, and the next instant, the Rat knew he was not quite so important as an Elephant.

A resemblance to the great in some things does not make us great.

27. The Ants and the Grasshopper

One bright day in late autumn a family of Ants were bustling about in the warm sunshine, drying out the grain they had stored up during the summer, when a starving Grasshopper, his fiddle under his arm, came up and humbly begged for a bite to eat.

"What!" cried the Ants in surprise, "haven't you stored anything away for the

winter? What in the world were you doing all last summer?"

"I didn't have time to store up any food," whined the Grasshopper; "I was so busy making music that before I knew it the summer was gone."

The Ants shrugged their shoulders in disgust.

"Making music, were you?" they cried. "Very well; now dance!" And they turned their backs on the Grasshopper and went on with their work.

There's a time for work and a time for play.

28. The Boys and the Frogs

Some Boys were playing one day at the edge of a pond in which lived a family of Frogs. The Boys amused themselves by throwing stones into the pond so as to make them skip on top of the water. The stones were flying thick and fast and the Boys were enjoying themselves very much; but the poor Frogs in the pond were trembling with fear.

At last one of the Frogs, the oldest and bravest, put his head out of the water, and said, "Oh, please, dear children, stop your cruel play! Though it may be fun for you, it means death to us!"

Always stop to think whether your fun

may not be the cause of another's unhappiness.

29. The Ass Carrying the Image

A sacred Image was being carried to the temple. It was mounted on an Ass adorned with garlands and gorgeous trappings, and a grand procession of priests and pages followed it through the streets. As the Ass walked along, the people bowed their heads reverently or fell on their knees, and the Ass thought the honor was being paid to himself.

With his head full of this foolish idea, he became so puffed up with pride and vanity that he halted and started to bray loudly. But in the midst of his song, his driver guessed what the Ass had got into his head, and began to beat him unmercifully with a stick.

"Go along with you, you stupid Ass," he cried. "The honor is not meant for you but for the image you are carrying."

Do not try to take the credit to yourself that is due to others.

30. The Raven and the Swan

A Raven, which you know is black as coal, was envious of the Swan, because her feathers were as white as the purest snow. The foolish bird got the idea that if he lived like the Swan, swimming and diving all day long and eating the weeds and plants that grow in the water, his feathers would turn white like the Swan's.

So he left his home in the woods and fields and flew down to live on the lakes and in the marshes. But though he washed and washed all day long, almost drowning himself at it, his feathers remained as black as ever. And as the water weeds he ate did not agree with him, he got thinner and thinner, and at last he died.

A change of habits will not alter nature.

31. The Two Goats

Two Goats, frisking gayly on the rocky steeps of a mountain valley, chanced to meet, one on each side of a deep chasm through which poured a mighty mountain torrent.

The trunk of a fallen tree formed the only means of crossing the chasm, and on this not even two squirrels could have passed each other in safety. The narrow path would have made the bravest tremble. Not so our Goats. Their pride would not permit either to stand aside for the other.

One set her foot on the log. The other did likewise. In the middle they met horn to horn. Neither would give way, and so they both fell, to be swept away by the roaring torrent below.

It is better to yield than to come to misfortune through stubbornness.

32. The Ass and the Load of Salt

A Merchant, driving his Ass homeward from the seashore with a heavy load of salt, came to a river crossed by a shallow ford. They had crossed this river many times before without accident, but this time the Ass slipped and fell when halfway over. And when the Merchant at last got him to his feet, much of the salt had melted away. Delighted to find how much lighter his burden had become, the Ass finished the journey very gayly.

Next day the Merchant went for another load of salt. On the way home the Ass, remembering what had happened at the ford, purposely let himself fall into the water, and again got rid of most of his burden. The angry Merchant immediately turned about and drove the Ass back to the seashore, where he loaded him with two great baskets of sponges. At the ford the Ass again tumbled over; but when he had scrambled to his feet, it was a very disconsolate Ass that dragged himself homeward under a load ten times heavier than before.

The same measures will not suit all circumstances.

33. The Leap at Rhodes

A certain man who visited foreign lands could talk of little when he returned to his home except the wonderful adventures he had met with and the great deeds he had done abroad.

One of the feats he told about was a leap he had made in a city Called Rhodes. That leap was so great, he said, that no other man could leap anywhere near the distance. A great many persons in Rhodes had seen him do it and would prove that what he told was true.

"No need of witnesses," said one of the hearers. "Suppose this city is Rhodes. Now show us how far you can jump."

Deeds count, not boasting words.

34. The Cock and the Jewel

A Cock was busily scratching and scraping about to find something to eat for himself and his family, when he happened to turn up a precious jewel that had been lost by its owner.

"Aha!" said the Cock. "No doubt you are very costly and he who lost you would give a great deal to find you. But as for me, I would choose a single grain of barleycorn before all the jewels in the world."

Precious things are without value to those who cannot prize them.

35. The Wild Boar and the Fox

A Wild Boar was sharpening his tusks busily against the stump of a tree, when a Fox happened by. Now the Fox was always looking for a chance to make fun of his neighbors. So he made a great show of looking anxiously about, as if in fear of some hidden enemy. But the Boar kept right on with his work.

"Why are you doing that?" asked the Fox at last with a grin. "There isn't any danger that I can see."

"True enough," replied the Boar, "but when danger does come there will not be time for such work as this. My weapons will have to be ready for use then, or I shall suffer for it."

Preparedness for war is the best guarantee of peace.

36. The Ass, the Fox, and the Lion

An Ass and a Fox had become close comrades, and were constantly in each other's company. While the Ass cropped a fresh bit of greens, the Fox would devour a chicken from the neighboring farmyard or a bit of cheese filched from the dairy.

One day the pair unexpectedly met a Lion. The Ass was very much frightened, but the Fox calmed his fears. "I will talk to him," he said. So the Fox walked boldly up to the Lion.

"Your highness," he said in an undertone, so the Ass could not hear him, "I've got a fine scheme in my head. If you promise not to hurt me, I will lead that foolish creature yonder into a pit where he can't get out, and you can feast at your pleasure."

The Lion agreed and the Fox returned to the Ass.

"I made him promise not to hurt us," said the Fox. "But come, I know a good place to hide till he is gone."

So the Fox led the Ass into a deep pit. But when the Lion saw that the Ass was his for the taking, he first of all struck down the traitor Fox.

Traitors may expect treachery.

37

The Birds, the Beasts, and the Bat

The Birds and the Beasts declared war against each other. No compromise was possible, and so they went at it tooth and claw. It is said the quarrel grew out of the persecution the race of Geese suffered at the teeth of the Fox family.

The Beasts, too, had cause for fight. The Eagle was constantly pouncing on the Hare, and the Owl dined daily on Mice. It was a terrible battle. Many a Hare and many a Mouse died. Chickens and Geese fell by the score—and the victor always stopped for a feast.

Now the Bat family had not openly joined either side. They were a very politic race. So when they saw the Birds getting the better of it, they were Birds for all there was in it. But when the tide of battle turned, they immediately sided with the Beasts. When the battle was over, the conduct of the Bats was discussed at the peace conference.

Such deceit was unpardonable, and Birds and Beasts made common cause to drive out the Bats. And since then the Bat family hides in dark towers and deserted ruins, flying out only in the night.

The deceitful have no friends.

38
The Lion, the Bear, and the Fox

Just as a great Bear rushed to seize a stray kid, a Lion leaped from another direction upon the same prey. The two fought furiously for the prize until they had received so many wounds that both sank down unable to continue the battle.

Just then a Fox dashed up, and seizing the kid, made off with it as fast as he could go, while the Lion and the Bear looked on in helpless rage.

"How much better it would have been," they said, "to have shared in a friendly spirit."

Those who have all the toil do not always get the profit.

39. The Wolf and the Lamb

A stray Lamb stood drinking early one morning on the bank of a woodland stream. That very same morning a hungry Wolf came by farther up the stream, hunting for something to eat. He soon got his eyes on the Lamb. As a rule Mr. Wolf snapped up such delicious morsels without making any bones about it, but this Lamb looked so very helpless and innocent that the Wolf felt he ought to have some kind of an excuse for taking its life.

"How dare you paddle around in my stream and stir up all the mud!" he shouted fiercely. "You deserve to be punished severely for your rashness!"

"But, your highness," replied the trembling Lamb, "do not be angry! I cannot possibly muddy the water you are drinking up there. Remember, you are upstream and I am downstream."

"You do muddy it!" retorted the Wolf savagely. "And besides, I have heard that you told lies about me last year!"

"How could I have done so?" pleaded the Lamb. "I wasn't born until this year."

"If it wasn't you, it was your brother!"

"I have no brothers."

"Well, then," snarled the Wolf, "It was someone in your family anyway. But no matter who it was, I do not intend to be talked out of my breakfast."

And without more words the Wolf seized the poor Lamb and carried her off to the forest.

The tyrant can always find an excuse for his

tyranny.

The unjust will not listen to the reasoning of the innocent.

40. The Monkey and the Camel

At a great celebration in honor of King Lion, the Monkey was asked to dance for the company. His dancing was very clever indeed, and the animals were all highly pleased with his grace and lightness.

The praise that was showered on the Monkey made the Camel envious. He was very sure that he could dance quite as well as the Monkey, if not better, so he pushed his way into the crowd that was gathered around the Monkey, and rising on his hind legs, began to dance. But the big hulking Camel made himself very ridiculous as he kicked out his knotty legs and twisted his long clumsy neck. Besides, the animals found it hard to keep their toes from under his heavy

hoofs.

At last, when one of his huge feet came within an inch of King Lion's nose, the animals were so disgusted that they set upon the Camel in a rage and drove him out into the desert. Shortly afterward, refreshments, consisting mostly of Camel's hump and ribs, were served to the company.

Do not try to ape your betters.

41. The Hares and the Frogs

Hares, as you know, are very timid. The least shadow, sends them scurrying in fright to a hiding place. Once they decided to die rather than live in such misery.

But while they were debating how best to meet death, they thought they heard a noise and in a flash were scampering off to the warren. On the way they passed a pond where a family of Frogs was sitting among the reeds on the bank. In an instant the startled Frogs were seeking safety in the mud.

"Look," cried a Hare, "things are not so bad after all, for here are creatures who are even afraid of us!"

However unfortunate we may think we are there is always someone worse off than ourselves.

42. The Travelers and the Sea

Two Travelers were walking along the seashore. Far out they saw something riding on the waves.

"Look," said one, "a great ship rides in from distant lands, bearing rich treasures!"

The object they saw came ever nearer the shore.

"No," said the other, "that is not a treasure ship. That is some fisherman's skiff, with the day's catch of savoury fish."

Still nearer came the object. The waves washed it up on shore.

"It is a chest of gold lost from some wreck," they cried. Both Travelers rushed to the beach, but there they found nothing but a water-soaked log.

Do not let your hopes carry you away from reality.

43. The Wolf and the Lion

A Wolf had stolen a Lamb and was carrying it off to his lair to eat it. But his plans were very much changed when he met a Lion, who, without making any excuses, took the Lamb away from him. The Wolf made off to a safe distance, and then said in a much injured tone:

"You have no right to take my property like that!"

The Lion looked back, but as the Wolf was too far away to be taught a lesson without too much inconvenience, he said:

"Your property? Did you buy it, or did the Shepherd make you a gift of it? Pray tell me, how did you get it?"

What is evil won is evil lost.

44. The Stag and His Reflection

A Stag, drinking from a crystal spring, saw himself mirrored in the clear water. He greatly admired the graceful arch of his antlers, but he was very much ashamed of his spindling legs.

"How can it be," he sighed, "that I should be cursed with such legs when I have so magnificent a crown."

At that moment he scented a panther and in an instant was bounding away through the forest. But as he ran his wide-spreading antlers caught in the branches of the trees, and soon the Panther overtook him. Then the Stag perceived that the legs of which he was so ashamed would have saved him had it not been for the useless ornaments on his head.

We often make much of the ornamental and despise the useful.

45. The Fox and the Stork

The Fox one day thought of a plan to amuse himself at the expense of the Stork, at whose odd appearance he was always laughing.

"You must come and dine with me today," he said to the Stork, smiling to himself at the trick he was going to play. The Stork gladly accepted the invitation and arrived in good time and with a very good appetite.

For dinner the Fox served soup. But it was set out in a very shallow dish, and all the Stork could do was to wet the very tip of his bill. Not a drop of soup could he get. But the Fox lapped it up easily, and, to increase the disappointment of the Stork, made a great show of enjoyment.

The hungry Stork was much displeased at the trick, but he was a calm, even-tempered fellow and saw no good in flying into a rage. Instead, not long afterward, he invited the Fox to dine with him in turn. The Fox arrived promptly at the time that had been set, and the Stork served a fish dinner that had a very appetizing smell. But it was served in a tall jar with a very narrow neck. The Stork could easily get at the food with his long

bill, but all the Fox could do was to lick the outside of the jar, and sniff at the delicious odor. And when the Fox lost his temper, the Stork said calmly:

"Do not play tricks on your neighbors unless you can stand the same treatment yourself."

Those who practice cunning must expect to suffer by it.

46. The Peacock

The Peacock, they say, did not at first have the beautiful feathers in which he now takes so much pride. These, Juno, whose favorite he was, granted to him one day when he begged her for a train of feathers to distinguish him from the other birds. Then, decked in his finery, gleaming with emerald, gold, purple, and azure, he strutted proudly among the birds. All regarded him with envy. Even the most beautiful pheasant could see that his beauty was surpassed.

Presently the Peacock saw an Eagle soaring high up in the blue sky and felt a desire to fly, as he had been accustomed to do. Lifting his wings he tried to rise from the ground. But the weight of his magnificent train held him down. Instead of flying up to greet the first rays of the morning sun or to bathe in the rosy light among the floating clouds at sunset, he would have to walk the ground more encumbered and oppressed than any common barnyard fowl.

Do not sacrifice your freedom for the sake of pomp and show.

47. The Mouse and the Bull

A Bull gave chase to a Mouse which had bitten him in the nose: but the Mouse was too quick for him and slipped into a hole in a wall. The Bull charged furiously into the wall again and again until he was tired out, and sank down on the ground exhausted with his efforts. When all was quiet, the Mouse darted out and bit him again.

Beside himself with rage he started to his feet, but by that time the Mouse was back in his hole again, and he could do nothing but bellow and fume in helpless anger. Presently he heard a shrill little voice say from inside the wall, "You big fellows don't always have it your own way, you see: sometimes we little ones come off best."

The battle is not always to the strong.

48. The Wolf and the Lean Dog

A Wolf prowling near a village one evening met a Dog. It happened to be a very lean and bony Dog, and Master Wolf would have turned up his nose at such meager fare had he not been more hungry than usual. So he began to edge toward the Dog, while the Dog backed away.

"Let me remind your lordship," said the Dog, his words interrupted now and then as he dodged a snap of the Wolf's teeth, "how unpleasant it would be to eat me now. Look at my ribs. I am nothing but skin and bone. But let me tell you something in private. In a few days my master will give a wedding feast for his only daughter. You can guess how fine and fat I will grow on the scraps from the table. Then is the time to eat me."

The Wolf could not help thinking how nice it would be to have a fine fat Dog to eat instead of the scrawny object before him. So he went away pulling in his belt and promising to return.

Some days later the Wolf came back for the promised feast. He found the Dog in his master's yard, and asked him to come out and be eaten.

"Sir," said the Dog, with a grin, "I shall be delighted to have you eat me. I'll be out as soon as the porter opens the door."

But the "porter" was a huge Dog whom the Wolf knew by painful experience to be very unkind toward wolves. So he decided not to wait and made off as fast as his legs could carry him.

Do not depend on the promises of those

whose interest it is to deceive you.
Take what you can get when you can get it.

49. The Dog and His Master's Dinner

A Dog had learned to carry his master's dinner to him every day. He was very faithful to his duty, though the smell of the good things in the basket tempted him.

The Dogs in the neighborhood noticed him carrying the basket and soon discovered what was in it. They made several attempts to steal it from him. But he always guarded it faithfully.

Then one day all the Dogs in the neighborhood got together and met him on his way with the basket. The Dog tried to run away from them. But at last he stopped to argue. That was his mistake. They soon made him feel so ridiculous that he dropped the basket and seized a large piece of roast meat intended for his master's dinner.

"Very well," he said, "you divide the rest."

Do not stop to argue with temptation.

50. The Fawn and His Mother

A Hind said to her Fawn, who was now well grown and strong, “My son, Nature has given you a powerful body and a stout pair of horns, and I can’t think why you are such a coward as to run away from the hounds.”

Just then they both heard the sound of a pack in full cry, but at a considerable distance. “You stay where you are,” said the Hind; “never mind me”: and with that she ran off as fast as her legs could carry her.

No arguments will give courage to the coward.

51. The Vain Jackdaw and His Borrowed Feathers

A Jackdaw chanced to fly over the garden of the King's palace. There he saw with much wonder and envy a flock of royal Peacocks in all the glory of their splendid plumage. Now the black Jackdaw was not a very handsome bird, nor very refined in manner.

Yet he imagined that all he needed to make himself fit for the society of the Peacocks was a dress like theirs. So he picked up some castoff feathers of the Peacocks and stuck them among his own black plumes. Dressed in his borrowed finery he strutted loftily among the birds of his own kind. Then he flew down into the garden among the Peacocks. But they soon saw who he was. Angry at the cheat, they flew at him, plucking away the borrowed feathers and also some of his own.

The poor Jackdaw returned sadly to his former companions. There another unpleasant surprise awaited him. They had not forgotten his superior airs toward them, and, to punish him, they drove him away with a rain of pecks and jeers.

Borrowed feathers do not make fine birds.

52. The Monkey and the Dolphin

It happened once upon a time that a certain Greek ship bound for Athens was wrecked off the coast close to Piraeus, the port of Athens. Had it not been for the Dolphins, who at that time were very friendly toward mankind and especially toward Athenians, all would have perished.

But the Dolphins took the shipwrecked people on their backs and swam with them to shore. Now it was the custom among the Greeks to take their pet monkeys and dogs with them whenever they went on a voyage. So when one of the Dolphins saw a Monkey struggling in the water, he thought it was a man, and made the Monkey climb up on his back. Then off he swam with him toward the

shore. The Monkey sat up, grave and dignified, on the Dolphin's back.

"You are a citizen of illustrious Athens, are you not?" asked the Dolphin politely.

"Yes," answered the Monkey, proudly. "My family is one of the noblest in the city."

"Indeed," said the Dolphin. "Then of course you often visit Piraeus."

"Yes, yes," replied the Monkey. "Indeed, I do. I am with him constantly. Piraeus is my very best friend."

This answer took the Dolphin by surprise, and, turning his head, he now saw what it was he was carrying. Without more ado, he dived and left the foolish Monkey to take care of himself, while he swam off in search of some human being to save.

One falsehood leads to another.

53. The Wolf and the Ass

An Ass was feeding in a pasture near a wood when he saw a Wolf lurking in the shadows along the hedge. He easily guessed what the Wolf had in mind, and thought of a plan to save himself. So he pretended he was lame, and began to hobble painfully.

When the Wolf came up, he asked the Ass what had made him lame, and the Ass replied that he had stepped on a sharp thorn.

"Please pull it out," he pleaded, groaning as if in pain. "If you do not, it might stick in your throat when you eat me."

The Wolf saw the wisdom of the advice, for he wanted to enjoy his meal without any danger of choking. So the Ass lifted up his foot and the Wolf began to search very closely and carefully for the thorn.

Just then the Ass kicked out with all his might, tumbling the Wolf a dozen paces away. And while the Wolf was getting very slowly and painfully to his feet, the Ass galloped away in safety.

"Serves me right," growled the Wolf as he crept into the bushes. "I'm a butcher by trade, not a doctor."

Stick to your trade.

54. The Monkey and the Cat

Once upon a time a Cat and a Monkey lived as pets in the same house. They were great friends and were constantly in all sorts of mischief together. What they seemed to think of more than anything else was to get something to eat, and it did not matter much to them how they got it.

One day they were sitting by the fire, watching some chestnuts roasting on the hearth. How to get them was the question.

"I would gladly get them," said the cunning Monkey, "but you are much more skillful at such things than I am. Pull them out and I'll divide them between us."

Pussy stretched out her paw very carefully, pushed aside some of the cinders, and drew back her paw very quickly. Then she tried it again, this time pulling a chestnut half out of the fire. A third time and she drew out the chestnut.

This performance she went through several times, each time singeing her paw severely. As fast as she pulled the chestnuts out of the fire, the Monkey ate them up.

Now the master came in, and away scampered the rascals, Mistress Cat with a burnt paw and no chestnuts. From that time on, they say, she contented herself with mice and rats and had little to do with Sir Monkey.

The flatterer seeks some benefit at your expense.

55. The Dogs and the Fox

Some Dogs found the skin of a Lion and furiously began to tear it with their teeth. A Fox chanced to see them and laughed scornfully.

"If that Lion had been alive," he said, "it would have been a very different story. He would have made you feel how much sharper his claws are than your teeth."

It is easy and also contemptible to kick a man that is down.

56. The Dogs and the Hides

Some hungry Dogs saw a number of hides at the bottom of a stream where the Tanner had put them to soak. A fine hide makes an excellent meal for a hungry Dog, but the water was deep and the Dogs could not reach the hides from the bank. So they held a council and decided that the very best thing to do was to drink up the river.

All fell to lapping up the water as fast as they could. But though they drank and drank until, one after another, all of them had burst with drinking, still, for all their effort, the water in the river remained as high as ever.

Do not try to do impossible things.

57. The Rabbit, the Weasel, and the Cat

A Rabbit left his home one day for a dinner of clover. But he forgot to latch the door of his house and while he was gone a Weasel walked in and calmly made himself at home. When the Rabbit returned, there was the Weasel's nose sticking out of the Rabbit's own doorway, sniffing the fine air. The Rabbit was quite angry—for a Rabbit—, and requested the Weasel to move out. But the Weasel was perfectly content. He was settled down for good.

A wise old Cat heard the dispute and offered to settle it.

"Come close to me," said the Cat, "I am very deaf. Put your mouths close to my ears while you tell me the facts."

The unsuspecting pair did as they were told and in an instant the Cat had them both under her claws. No one could deny that the dispute had been definitely settled.

The strong are apt to settle questions to their own advantage.

58. The Bear and the Bees

A Bear roaming the woods in search of berries happened on a fallen tree in which a swarm of Bees had stored their honey. The Bear began to nose around the log very carefully to find out if the Bees were at home. Just then one of the swarm came home from the clover field with a load of sweets. Guessing what the Bear was after, the Bee flew at him, stung him sharply and then disăppeared into the hollow log.

The Bear lost his temper in an instant, and sprang upon the log tooth and claw, to destroy the nest. But this only brought out the whole swarm. The poor Bear had to take to his heels, and he was able to save himself only by diving into a pool of water.

It is wiser to bear a single injury in silence than to provoke a thousand by flying into a rage.

59. The Heron

A Heron was walking sedately along the bank of a stream, his eyes on the clear water, and his long neck and pointed bill ready to snap up a likely morsel for his breakfast. The clear water swarmed with fish, but Master Heron was hard to please that morning.

"No small fry for me," he said. "Such scanty fare is not fit for a Heron."

Now a fine young Perch swam near.

"No indeed," said the Heron. "I wouldn't even trouble to open my beak for anything like that!"

As the sun rose, the fish left the shallow water near the shore and swam below into the cool depths toward the middle. The Heron saw no more fish, and very glad was he at last to breakfast on a tiny Snail.

Do not be too hard to suit or you may have
to be content with
the worst or with nothing at all.

60. The Fox and the Leopard

A Fox and a Leopard, resting lazily after a generous dinner, amused themselves by disputing about their good looks. The Leopard was very proud of his glossy, spotted coat and made disdainful remarks about the Fox, whose appearance he declared was quite ordinary.

The Fox prided himself on his fine

bushy tail with its tip of white, but he was wise enough to see that he could not rival the Leopard in looks. Still he kept up a flow of sarcastic talk, just to exercise his wits and to have the fun of disputing. The Leopard was about to lose his temper when the Fox got up, yawning lazily.

"You may have a very smart coat," he said, "but you would be a great deal better off if you had a little more smartness inside your head and less on your ribs, the way I am. That's what I call real beauty."

A fine coat is not always an indication of an attractive mind.

61. The Cock and the Fox

One bright evening as the sun was sinking on a glorious world a wise old Cock flew into a tree to roost. Before he composed himself to rest, he flapped his wings three times and crowed loudly. But just as he was about to put his head under his wing, his beady eyes caught a flash of red and a glimpse of a long pointed nose, and there just below him stood Master Fox.

"Have you heard the wonderful news?" cried the Fox in a very joyful and excited manner.

"What news?" asked the Cock very calmly. But he had a queer, fluttery feeling inside him, for, you know, he was very much afraid of the Fox.

"Your family and mine and all other animals have agreed to forget their differences and live in peace and friendship from now on forever. Just think of it! I simply cannot wait to embrace you! Do come down, dear friend, and let us celebrate the joyful event."

"How grand!" said the Cock. "I certainly am delighted at the news." But he spoke in an absent way, and stretching up on tiptoes, seemed to be looking at something afar off.

"What is it you see?" asked the Fox a little anxiously.

"Why, it looks to me like a couple of Dogs coming this way. They must have heard the good news and—"

But the Fox did not wait to hear more. Off he started on a run.

"Wait," cried the Cock. "Why do you run? The Dogs are friends of yours now!"

"Yes," answered the Fox. "But they might not have heard the news. Besides, I have a very important errand that I had almost forgotten about."

The Cock smiled as he buried his head in his feathers and went to sleep, for he had succeeded in outwitting a very crafty enemy.

The trickster is easily tricked.

62. The Wolf and the Goat

A hungry Wolf spied a Goat browsing at the top of a steep cliff where he could not possibly get at her.

"That is a very dangerous place for you," he called out, pretending to be very anxious about the Goat's safety. "What if you should fall! Please listen to me and come down! Here you can get all you want of the finest, tenderest grass in the country."

The Goat looked over the edge of the cliff.

"How very, very anxious you are about me," she said, "and how generous you are with your grass! But I know you! It's your own appetite you are thinking of, not mine!"

An invitation prompted by selfishness is not to be accepted.

63. The Ass and the Grasshoppers

One day as an Ass was walking in the pasture, he found some Grasshoppers chirping merrily in a grassy corner of the field. He listened with a great deal of admiration to the song of the Grasshoppers. It was such a joyful song that his pleasure-loving heart was filled with a wish to sing as they did.

"What is it?" he asked very respectfully, "that has given you such beautiful voices? Is there any special food you eat, or is it some divine nectar that makes you sing so wonderfully?"

"Yes," said the Grasshoppers, who were very fond of a joke; "it is the dew we drink! Try some and see."

So thereafter the Ass would eat nothing

and drink nothing but dew. Naturally, the poor foolish Ass soon died.

The laws of nature are unchangeable.

64. The Fox and the Goat

A Fox fell into a well, and though it was not very deep, he found that he could not get out again. After he had been in the well a long time, a thirsty Goat came by. The Goat thought the Fox had gone down to drink, and so he asked if the water was good.

"The finest in the whole country," said the crafty Fox, "jump in and try it. There is more than enough for both of us."

The thirsty Goat immediately jumped in and began to drink. The Fox just as quickly jumped on the Goat's back and leaped from the tip of the Goat's horns out of the well. The foolish Goat now saw what a plight he had got into, and begged the Fox to help him out. But the Fox was already on his way to the woods.

"If you had as much sense as you have beard, old fellow," he said as he ran, "you would have been more cautious about finding a way to get out again before you jumped in."

Look before you leap.

65. The Cat, the Cock, and the Young Mouse

A very young Mouse, who had never seen anything of the world, almost came to grief the very first time he ventured out. And this is the story he told his mother about his adventures.

"I was strolling along very peaceably when, just as I turned the corner into the next yard, I saw two strange creatures. One of them had a very kind and gracious look, but the other was the most fearful monster you can imagine. You should have seen him.

"On top of his head and in front of his neck hung pieces of raw red meat. He walked about restlessly, tearing up the ground with his toes, and beating his arms savagely against his sides. The moment he caught sight of me he opened his pointed mouth as if to swallow me, and then he let out a piercing roar that frightened me almost to death."

Can you guess who it was that our young Mouse was trying to describe to his mother? It was nobody but the Barnyard Cock and the first one the little Mouse had ever seen.

"If it had not been for that terrible monster," the Mouse went on, "I should have made the acquaintance of the pretty creature, who looked so good and gentle. He had thick, velvety fur, a meek face, and a look that was very modest, though his eyes were bright and shining. As he looked at me he waved his fine long tail and smiled.

"I am sure he was just about to speak to me when the monster I have told you about let out a screaming yell, and I ran for my life."

"My son," said the Mother Mouse, "that gentle creature you saw was none other than the Cat. Under his kindly appearance, he bears a grudge against every one of us. The other was nothing but a bird who wouldn't harm you in the least. As for the Cat, he eats us. So be thankful, my child, that you escaped with your life, and, as long as you live, never judge people by their looks."

Do not trust alone to outward appearances.

66. The Wolf and the Shepherd

A Wolf had been prowling around a flock of Sheep for a long time, and the Shepherd watched very anxiously to prevent him from carrying off a Lamb. But the Wolf did not try to do any harm. Instead he seemed to be helping the Shepherd take care of the Sheep. At last the Shepherd got so used to seeing the Wolf about that he forgot how wicked he could be.

One day he even went so far as to leave his flock in the Wolf's care while he went on an errand. But when he came back and saw how many of the flock had been killed and carried off, he knew how foolish to trust a Wolf.

Once a wolf, always a wolf.

67. The Peacock and the Crane

A Peacock, puffed up with vanity, met a Crane one day, and to impress him spread his gorgeous tail in the Sun.

"Look," he said. "What have you to compare with this? I am dressed in all the glory of the rainbow, while your feathers are gray as dust!"

The Crane spread his broad wings and flew up toward the sun.

"Follow me if you can," he said. But the Peacock stood where he was among the birds of the barnyard, while the Crane soared in freedom far up into the blue sky.

The useful is of much more importance and

value,
than the ornamental.

68. The Farmer and the Cranes

Some Cranes saw a farmer plowing a large field. When the work of plowing was done, they patiently watched him sow the seed. It was their feast, they thought.

So, as soon as the Farmer had finished planting and had gone home, down they flew to the field, and began to eat as fast as they could.

The Farmer, of course, knew the Cranes and their ways. He had had experience with such birds before. He soon returned to the field with a sling. But he did not bring any stones with him. He expected to scare the Cranes just by swinging the sling in the air, and shouting loudly at them.

At first the Cranes flew away in great

terror. But they soon began to see that none of them ever got hurt. They did not even hear the noise of stones whizzing through the air, and as for words, they would kill nobody. At last they paid no attention whatever to the Farmer.

The Farmer saw that he would have to take other measures. He wanted to save at least some of his grain. So he loaded his sling with stones and killed several of the Cranes.

This had the effect the Farmer wanted, for from that day the Cranes visited his field no more.

Bluff and threatening words are of little value with rascals.
Bluff is no proof that hard fists are lacking.

69. The Dog in the Manger

A Dog asleep in a manger filled with hay, was awakened by the Cattle, which came in tired and hungry from working in the field. But the Dog would not let them get near the manger, and snarled and snapped as if it were filled with the best of meat and bones, all for himself. The Cattle looked at

the Dog in disgust.

"How selfish he is!" said one. "He cannot eat the hay and yet he will not let us eat it who are so hungry for it!"

Now the farmer came in. When he saw how the Dog was acting, he seized a stick and drove him out of the stable with many a blow for his selfish behavior.

Do not grudge others what you cannot enjoy yourself.

70. The Farmer and His Sons

A rich old farmer, who felt that he had not many more days to live, called his sons to his bedside.

"My sons," he said, "heed what I have to say to you. Do not on any account part with the estate that has belonged to our family for so many generations. Somewhere on it is hidden a rich treasure. I do not know the exact spot, but it is there, and you will surely find it. Spare no energy and leave no spot unturned in your search."

The father died, and no sooner was he in his grave than the sons set to work digging with all their might, turning up every foot of ground with their spades, and going over the whole farm two or three times. No hidden gold did they find; but at harvest time when they had settled their accounts and had pocketed a rich profit far greater than that of any of their neighbors, they understood that the treasure their father had told them about was the wealth of a bountiful crop, and that in their industry had they found the treasure.

Industry is itself a treasure.

71. The Two Pots

Two Pots, one of brass and the other of clay, stood together on the hearthstone. One day the Brass Pot proposed to the Earthen Pot that they go out into the world together. But the Earthen Pot excused himself, saying that it would be wiser for him to stay in the corner by the fire.

"It would take so little to break me," he said. "You know how fragile I am. The least shock is sure to shatter me!"

"Don't let that keep you at home," urged the Brass Pot. "I shall take very good care of you. If we should happen to meet anything hard I will step between and save you."

So the Earthen Pot at last consented, and the two set out side by side, jolting along on three stubby legs first to this side, then to that, and bumping into each other at every step.

The Earthen Pot could not survive that sort of companionship very long. They had not gone ten paces before the Earthen Pot cracked, and at the next jolt he flew into a thousand pieces.

Equals make the best friends.

72. The Goose and the Golden Egg

There was once a Countryman who possessed the most wonderful Goose you can imagine, for every day when he visited the nest, the Goose had laid a beautiful, glittering, golden egg. The Countryman took the eggs to market and soon began to get rich. But it was not long before he grew impatient with the Goose because she gave him only a single golden egg a day. He was not getting rich fast enough.

Then one day, after he had finished counting his money, the idea came to him that he could get all the golden eggs at once by killing the Goose and cutting it open.

But when the deed was done, not a single golden egg did he find, and his precious

Goose was dead.

Those who have plenty want more and so lose all they have.

73. The Fighting Bulls and the Frog

Two Bulls were fighting furiously in a field, at one side of which was a marsh. An old Frog living in the marsh, trembled as he watched the fierce battle.

"What are you afraid of?" asked a young Frog.

"Do you not see," replied the old Frog, "that the Bull who is beaten, will be driven away from the good forage up there to the reeds of this marsh, and we shall all be trampled into the mud?"

It turned out as the Frog had said. The beaten Bull was driven to the marsh, where his great hoofs crushed the Frogs to death.

When the great fall out, the weak must suffer for it.

74. The Mouse and the Weasel

A little hungry Mouse found his way one day into a basket of corn. He had to squeeze himself a good deal to get through the narrow opening between the strips of the basket. But the corn was tempting and the Mouse was determined to get in. When at last he had succeeded, he gorged himself to bursting. Indeed he he became about three times as big around the middle as he was when he went in.

At last he felt satisfied and dragged himself to the opening to get out again. But the best he could do was to get his head out.

So there he sat groaning and moaning, both from the discomfort inside him and his anxiety to escape from the basket.

Just then a Weasel came by. He understood the situation quickly.

"My friend," he said, "I know what you've been doing. You've been stuffing. That's what you get. You will have to stay there till you feel just like you did when you went in. Good night, and good enough for you."

And that was all the sympathy the poor Mouse got.

Greediness leads to misfortune.

75. The Farmer and the Snake

A Farmer walked through his field one cold winter morning. On the ground lay a Snake, stiff and frozen with the cold. The Farmer knew how deadly the Snake could be, and yet he picked it up and put it in his bosom to warm it back to life.

The Snake soon revived, and when it had enough strength, bit the man who had been so kind to it. The bite was deadly and the Farmer felt that he must die. As he drew his last breath, he said to those standing around:

"Learn from my fate not to take pity on a scoundrel."

Kindness to ungrateful and vicious creatures is thrown away.

76. The Sick Stag

A Stag had fallen sick. He had just strength enough to gather some food and find a quiet clearing in the woods, where he lay down to wait until his strength should return. The Animals heard about the Stag's illness and came to ask after his health. Of course, they were all hungry, and helped themselves freely to the Stag's food; and as you would expect, the Stag soon starved to death.

Good will is worth nothing unless it is accompanied by good acts.

77. The Goatherd and the Wild Goats

One cold stormy day a Goatherd drove his Goats for shelter into a cave, where a number of Wild Goats had also found their way. The Shepherd wanted to make the Wild Goats part of his flock; so he fed them well. But to his own flock, he gave only just enough food to keep them alive. When the weather cleared, and the Shepherd led the Goats out to feed, the Wild Goats scampered off to the hills.

"Is that the thanks I get for feeding you and treating you so well?" complained the Shepherd.

"Do not expect us to join your flock," replied one of the Wild Goats. "We know how you would treat us later on, if some strangers should come as we did."

It is unwise to treat old friends badly for the sake of new ones.

78. The Spendthrift and the Swallow

A young fellow, who was very popular among his boon companions as a good spender, quickly wasted his fortune trying to live up to his reputation.

Then one fine day in early spring he found himself with not a penny left, and no property save the clothes he wore. He was to meet some jolly young men that morning, and he was at his wits' end how to get enough money to keep up appearances.

Just then a Swallow flew by, twittering merrily, and the young man, thinking summer had come, hastened off to a clothes dealer, to whom he sold all the clothes he wore down to his very tunic.

A few days later a change in weather

brought a severe frost; and the poor swallow and that foolish young man in his light tunic, and with his arms and knees bare, could scarcely keep life in their shivering bodies.

One swallow does not make a summer.

79. The Dog and the Oyster

There was once a Dog who was very fond of eggs. He visited the hen house very often and at last got so greedy that he would swallow the eggs whole.

One day the Dog wandered down to the seashore. There he spied an Oyster. In a twinkling the Oyster was resting in the Dog's stomach, shell and all. It pained the Dog a good deal, as you can guess.

"I've learned that all round things are not eggs," he said groaning.

Act in haste and repent at leisure—and often in pain.

80. Three Bullocks and a Lion

A Lion had been watching three Bullocks feeding in an open field. He had tried to attack them several times, but they had kept together, and helped each other to drive him off.

The Lion had little hope of eating them, for he was no match for three strong Bullocks with their sharp horns and hoofs. But he could not keep away from that field, for it is hard to resist watching a good meal, even when there is little chance of getting it.

Then one day the Bullocks had a quarrel, and when the hungry Lion came to look at them and lick his chops as he was accustomed to do, he found them in separate corners of the field, as far away from one another as they could get. It was now an easy matter for the Lion to attack them one at a time, and this he proceeded to do with the greatest satisfaction and relish.

In unity is strength.

81. The Cat and the Birds

A Cat was growing very thin. As you have guessed, he did not get enough to eat.

One day he heard that some Birds in the neighborhood were ailing and needed a doctor. So he put on a pair of spectacles, and with a leather box in his hand, knocked at the door of the Bird's home. The Birds peeped out, and Dr. Cat, with much solicitude, asked how they were. He would be very happy to give them some medicine.

"Tweet, tweet," laughed the Birds. "Very smart, aren't you? We are very well, thank you, and more so, if you only keep away from here."

Be wise and shun the quack.

82. The Astrologer

A man who lived a long time ago believed that he could read the future in the stars. He called himself an Astrologer, and spent his time at night gazing at the sky.

One evening he was walking along the open road outside the village. His eyes were fixed on the stars. He thought he saw there that the end of the world was at hand, when all at once, down he went into a hole full of mud and water. There he stood up to his ears, in the muddy water, and madly clawing at the slippery sides of the hole in his effort to climb out. His cries for help soon brought the villagers running. As they pulled him out of the mud, one of them said:

"You pretend to read the future in the

stars, and yet you fail to see what is at your feet! This may teach you to pay more attention to what is right in front of you, and let the future take care of itself."

"What use is it," said another, "to read the stars, when you can't see what's right here on the earth?"

Take care of the little things and the big things will take care of themselves.

83. Mercury and the Woodman

A poor Woodman was cutting down a tree near the edge of a deep pool in the forest. It was late in the day and the Woodman was tired. He had been working since sunrise and his strokes were not so sure as they had been early that morning. Thus it happened that the axe slipped and flew out of his hands into the pool. The Woodman was in despair. The axe was all he possessed with which to make a living, and he had not money enough to buy a new one.

As he stood wringing his hands and weeping, the god Mercury suddenly appeared and asked what the trouble was. The Woodman told what had happened, and straightway the kind Mercury dived into the pool. When he came up again he held a wonderful golden axe.

"Is this your axe?" Mercury asked the Woodman.

"No," answered the honest Woodman, "that is not my axe."

Mercury laid the golden axe on the bank and sprang back into the pool. This time he brought up an axe of silver, but the Woodman declared again that his axe was just an ordinary one with a wooden handle. Mercury dived down for the third time, and when he came up again he had the very axe that had been lost. The poor Woodman was very glad that his axe had been found and could not thank the kind god enough. Mercury was greatly pleased with the Woodman's honesty.

"I admire your honesty," he said, "and as a reward you may have all three axes, the gold and the silver as well as your own."

The happy Woodman returned to his home with his treasures, and soon the story of his good fortune was known to everybody in the village. Now there were several Woodmen in the village who believed that they could easily win the same good fortune. They hurried out into the woods, one here, one there, and hiding their axes in the bushes, pretended they had lost them. Then they wept and wailed and called on Mercury to help them.

And indeed, Mercury did appear, first to this one, then to that. To each one he showed an axe of gold, and each one eagerly claimed it to be the one he had lost. But Mercury did not give them the golden axe. Oh no! Instead he gave them each a hard whack over the head with it and sent them home. And when they returned next day to look for their own axes, they were nowhere to be found.

Honesty is the best policy.

84. The Frog and the Mouse

A young Mouse in search of adventure was running along the bank of a pond where lived a Frog. When the Frog saw the Mouse, he swam to the bank and croaked:

"Won't you pay me a visit? I can promise you a good time if you do."

The Mouse did not need much coaxing, for he was very anxious to see the world and everything in it. But though he could swim a little, he did not dare risk going into the pond without some help. The Frog had a plan. He tied the Mouse's leg to his own with a tough reed. Then into the pond he jumped, dragging his foolish companion with him.

The Mouse soon had enough of it and wanted to return to shore; but the treacherous

Frog had other plans. He pulled the Mouse down under the water and drowned him.

But before he could untie the reed that bound him to the dead Mouse, a Hawk came sailing over the pond.

Seeing the body of the Mouse floating on the water, the Hawk swooped down, seized the Mouse and carried it off, with the Frog dangling from its leg.

Thus at one swoop he had caught both meat and fish for his dinner.

Those who seek to harm others often come
to harm themselves
through their own deceit.

85. The Fox and the Crab

A Crab one day grew disgusted with the sands in which he lived. He decided to take a stroll to the meadow not far inland. There he would find better fare than briny water and sand mites.

So off he crawled to the meadow. But there a hungry Fox spied him, and in a twinkling, ate him up, both shell and claw.

Be content with your lot.

86. The Serpent and the Eagle

A Serpent had succeeded in surprising an Eagle and had wrapped himself around the Eagle's neck. The Eagle could not reach the Serpent, neither with beak nor claws. Far into the sky he soared trying to shake off his enemy. But the Serpent's hold only tightened, and slowly the Eagle sank back to earth, gasping for breath.

A Countryman chanced to see the unequal combat. In pity for the noble Eagle he rushed up and soon had loosened the coiling Serpent and freed the Eagle. The Serpent was furious. He had no chance to bite the watchful Countryman. Instead he struck at the drinking horn, hanging at the Countryman's belt, and into it let fly the poison of his fangs.

The Countryman now went on toward home. Becoming thirsty on the way, he filled his horn at a spring, and was about to drink. There was a sudden rush of great wings. Sweeping down, the Eagle seized the poisoned horn from out his savior's hands, and flew away with it to hide it where it could never be found.

An act of kindness is well repaid.

87. The Wolf and His Shadow

A Wolf left his lair one evening in fine spirits and an excellent appetite. As he ran, the setting sun cast his shadow far out on the ground, and it looked as if the wolf were a hundred times bigger than he really was.

"Why," exclaimed the Wolf proudly, "see how big I am! Fancy me running away from a puny Lion! I'll show him who is fit to be king, he or I."

Just then an immense shadow blotted him out entirely, and the next instant a Lion struck him down with a single blow.

Do not let your fancy make you forget realities.

88. The Wolf in Sheep's Clothing

A certain Wolf could not get enough to eat because of the watchfulness of the Shepherds. But one night he found a sheep skin that had been cast aside and forgotten. The next day, dressed in the skin, the Wolf strolled into the pasture with the Sheep. Soon a little Lamb was following him about and was quickly led away to slaughter.

That evening the Wolf entered the fold with the flock. But it happened that the Shepherd took a fancy for mutton broth that very evening, and, picking up a knife, went to the fold. There the first he laid hands on and killed was the Wolf.

The evil doer often comes to harm through his own deceit.

89. The Bull and the Goat

A Bull once escaped from a Lion by entering a cave which the Goatherds used to house their flocks in stormy weather and at night. It happened that one of the Goats had been left behind, and the Bull had no sooner got inside than this Goat lowered his head and made a rush at him, butting him with his horns. As the Lion was still prowling outside the entrance to the cave, the Bull had to submit to the insult.

"Do not think," he said, "that I submit to your cowardly treatment because I am afraid of you. When that Lion leaves, I'll teach you a lesson you won't forget."

It is wicked to take advantage of another's distress.

90. The Eagle and the Beetle

A Beetle once begged the Eagle to spare a Hare which had run to her for protection. But the Eagle pounced upon her prey, the sweep of her great wings tumbling the Beetle a dozen feet away. Furious at the disrespect shown her, the Beetle flew to the Eagle's nest and rolled out the eggs. Not one did she spare. The Eagle's grief and anger knew no bounds, but who had done the cruel deed she did not know.

Next year the Eagle built her nest far up on a mountain crag; but the Beetle found it and again destroyed the eggs. In despair the Eagle now implored great Jupiter to let her place her eggs in his lap. There none would dare harm them. But the Beetle buzzed about

Jupiter's head, and made him rise to drive her away; and the eggs rolled from his lap.

Now the Beetle told the reason for her action, and Jupiter had to acknowledge the justice of her cause. And they say that ever after, while the Eagle's eggs lie in the nest in spring, the Beetle still sleeps in the ground. For so Jupiter commanded.

Even the weakest may find means to avenge a wrong.

91. The Old Lion and the Fox

An old Lion, whose teeth and claws were so worn that it was not so easy for him to get food as in his younger days, pretended that he was sick. He took care to let all his neighbors know about it, and then lay down in his cave to wait for visitors. And when they came to offer him their sympathy, he ate them up one by one.

The Fox came too, but he was very cautious about it. Standing at a safe distance from the cave, he inquired politely after the Lion's health. The Lion replied that he was very ill indeed, and asked the Fox to step in for a moment. But Master Fox very wisely stayed outside, thanking the Lion very kindly for the invitation.

"I should be glad to do as you ask," he added, "but I have noticed that there are many footprints leading into your cave and none coming out. Pray tell me, how do your visitors find their way out again?"

Take warning from the misfortunes of others.

92. The Man and the Lion

A Lion and a Man chanced to travel in company through the forest. They soon began to quarrel, for each of them boasted that he and his kind were far superior to the other both in strength and mind.

Now they reached a clearing in the forest and there stood a statue. It was a representation of Heracles in the act of tearing the jaws of the Nemean Lion.

"See," said the man, "that's how strong we are! The King of Beasts is like wax in our hands!"

"Ho!" laughed the Lion, "a Man made that statue. It would have been quite a different scene had a Lion made it!"

It all depends on the point of view, and who tells the story.

93. The Ass and the Lap Dog

There was once an Ass whose Master also owned a Lap Dog. This Dog was a favorite and received many a pat and kind word from his Master, as well as choice bits from his plate. Every day the Dog would run to meet the Master, frisking playfully about and leaping up to lick his hands and face.

All this the Ass saw with much discontent. Though he was well fed, he had much work to do; besides, the Master hardly ever took any notice of him. Now the jealous Ass got it into his silly head that all he had to do to win his Master's favor was to act like the Dog.

So one day he left his stable and clattered eagerly into the house.Finding his

Master seated at the dinner table, he kicked up his heels and, with a loud bray, pranced giddily around the table, upsetting it as he did so. Then he planted his forefeet on his Master's knees and rolled out his tongue to lick the Master's face, as he had seen the Dog do.

But his weight upset the chair, and Ass and man rolled over together in the pile of broken dishes from the table. The Master was much alarmed at the strange behavior of the Ass, and calling for help, soon attracted the attention of the servants. When they saw the danger the Master was in from the clumsy beast, they set upon the Ass and drove him with kicks and blows back to the stable. There they left him to mourn the foolishness that had brought him nothing but a sound beating.

Behavior that is regarded as agreeable in one
is very rude
and impertinent in another.
Do not try to gain favor by acting in a way
that is contrary to
your own nature and character.

94. The Milkmaid and Her Pail

A Milkmaid had been out to milk the cows and was returning from the field with the shining milk pail balanced nicely on her head. As she walked along, her pretty head was busy with plans for the days to come.

'This good, rich milk,' she mused, 'will give me plenty of cream to churn. The butter I make I will take to market, and with the money I get for it I will buy a lot of eggs for hatching. How nice it will be when they are all hatched and the yard is full of fine young chicks. Then when May day comes I will sell them, and with the money I'll buy a lovely new dress to wear to the fair. All the young men will look at me. They will come and try to make love to me,— but I shall very quickly send them about their business!'

As she thought of how she would settle that matter, she tossed her head scornfully, and down fell the pail of milk to the ground. And all the milk flowed out, and with it vanished butter and eggs and chicks and new dress and all the milkmaid's pride.

Do not count your chickens before they are hatched.

95. The Stag with One Eye

A Stag, blind of one eye, was grazing close to the sea-shore and kept his sound eye turned towards the land, so as to be able to perceive the approach of the hounds, while the blind eye he turned towards the sea, never suspecting that any danger would threaten him from that quarter.

As it fell out, however, some sailors, coasting along the shore, spied him and shot an arrow at him, by which he was mortally wounded. As he lay dying, he said to himself, "Wretch that I am! I bethought me of the dangers of the land, whence none assailed me: but I feared no peril from the sea, yet thence has come my ruin."

Misfortune often assails us from an unexpected quarter.

96. The Miser

A Miser had buried his gold in a secret place in his garden. Every day he went to the spot, dug up the treasure and counted it piece by piece to make sure it was all there. He made so many trips that a Thief, who had been observing him, guessed what it was the Miser had hidden, and one night quietly dug up the treasure and made off with it.

When the Miser discovered his loss, he was overcome with grief and despair. He groaned and cried and tore his hair. A passerby heard his cries and asked what had happened.

"My gold! O my gold!" cried the Miser, wildly, "someone has robbed me!"

"Your gold! There in that hole? Why did

you put it there? Why did you not keep it in the house where you could easily get it when you had to buy things?"

"Buy!" screamed the Miser angrily. "Why, I never touched the gold. I couldn't think of spending any of it."

The stranger picked up a large stone and threw it into the hole.

"If that is the case," he said, "cover up that stone. It is worth just as much to you as the treasure you lost!"

A possession is worth no more than the use we make of it.

97. The Wolf and the House Dog

There was once a Wolf who got very little to eat because the Dogs of the village were so wide awake and watchful. He was really nothing but skin and bones, and it made him very downhearted to think of it.

One night this Wolf happened to fall in with a fine fat House Dog who had wandered a little too far from home. The Wolf would gladly have eaten him then and there, but the House Dog looked strong enough to leave his marks should he try it.

So the Wolf spoke very humbly to the Dog, complimenting him on his fine appearance.

"You can be as well-fed as I am if you want to," replied the Dog. "Leave the woods;

there you live miserably. Why, you have to fight hard for every bite you get. Follow my example and you will get along beautifully."

"What must I do?" asked the Wolf.

"Hardly anything," answered the House Dog. "Chase people who carry canes, bark at beggars, and fawn on the people of the house. In return you will get tidbits of every kind, chicken bones, choice bits of meat, sugar, cake, and much more beside, not to speak of kind words and caresses."

The Wolf had such a beautiful vision of his coming happiness that he almost wept. But just then he noticed that the hair on the Dog's neck was worn and the skin was chafed.

"What is that on your neck?"

"Nothing at all," replied the Dog.

"What! nothing!"

"Oh, just a trifle!"

"But please tell me."

"Perhaps you see the mark of the collar to which my chain is fastened."

"What! A chain!" cried the Wolf. "Don't you go wherever you please?"

"Not always! But what's the difference?" replied the Dog.

"All the difference in the world! I don't care a rap for your feasts and I wouldn't take all the tender young lambs in the world at that price." And away ran the Wolf to the woods.

There is nothing worth so much as liberty.

98. The Fox and the Hedgehog

A Fox, swimming across a river, was barely able to reach the bank, where he lay bruised and exhausted from his struggle with the swift current.

Soon a swarm of blood-sucking flies settled on him; but he lay quietly, still too weak to run away from them. A Hedgehog happened by. "Let me drive the flies away," he said kindly.

"No, no!" exclaimed the Fox, "do not disturb them! They have taken all they can hold. If you drive them away, another greedy swarm will come and take the little blood I have left."

Better to bear a lesser evil than to risk a greater in removing it.

99. The Bat and the Weasels

A Bat blundered into the nest of a Weasel, who ran up to catch and eat him. The Bat begged for his life, but the Weasel would not listen.

"You are a Mouse," he said, "and I am a sworn enemy of Mice. Every Mouse I catch, I am going to eat!"

"But I am not a Mouse!" cried the Bat. "Look at my wings. Can Mice fly? Why, I am only a Bird! Please let me go!"

The Weasel had to admit that the Bat was not a Mouse, so he let him go. But a few days later, the foolish Bat went blindly into the nest of another Weasel. This Weasel happened to be a bitter enemy of Birds, and he soon had the Bat under his claws, ready to eat him.

"You are a Bird," he said, "and I am going to eat you!"

"What," cried the Bat, "I, a Bird! Why, all Birds have feathers! I am nothing but a Mouse. 'Down with all Cats,' is my motto!"

And so the Bat escaped with his life a second time.

You should be equal to the occasion.

100. The Quack Toad

An old Toad once informed all his neighbors that he was a learned doctor. In fact he could cure anything. The Fox heard the news and hurried to see the Toad. He looked the Toad over very carefully.

"Mr. Toad," he said, "I've been told that you cure anything! But just take a look at yourself, and then try some of your own medicine. If you can cure yourself of that blotchy skin and that rheumatic gait, someone might believe you. Otherwise, I should advise you to try some other profession."

Those who would mend others, should first mend themselves.

101. The Fox without a Tail

A Fox that had been caught in a trap, succeeded at last, after much painful tugging, in getting away. But he had to leave his beautiful bushy tail behind him.

For a long time he kept away from the other Foxes, for he knew well enough that they would all make fun of him and crack jokes and laugh behind his back. But it was hard for him to live alone, and at last he

thought of a plan that would perhaps help him out of his trouble. He called a meeting of all the Foxes, saying that he had something of great importance to tell the tribe. When they were all gathered together, the Fox Without a Tail got up and made a long speech about those Foxes who had come to harm because of their tails. This one had been caught by hounds when his tail had become entangled in the hedge. That one had not been able to run fast enough because of the weight of his brush.

Besides, it was well known, he said, that men hunt Foxes simply for their tails, which they cut off as prizes of the hunt.

"With such proof of the danger and uselessness of having a tail," said Master Fox, "he would advise every Fox to cut it off, if he valued life and safety."

When he had finished talking, an old Fox arose, and said, smiling:

"Master Fox, kindly turn around for a moment, and you shall have your answer."

When the poor Fox Without a Tail turned around, there arose such a storm of jeers and hooting, that he saw how useless it was to try any longer to persuade the Foxes to part with their tails.

Do not listen to the advice of him who seeks to lower you to his own level.

102. The Mischievous Dog

There was once a Dog who was so ill-natured and mischievous that his Master had to fasten a heavy wooden clog about his neck to keep him from annoying visitors and neighbors. But the Dog seemed to be very proud of the clog and dragged it about noisily as if he wished to attract everybody's attention. He was not able to impress anyone.

"You would be wiser," said an old acquaintance, "to keep quietly out of sight with that clog. Do you want everybody to know what a disgraceful and ill-natured Dog you are?"

Notoriety is not fame.

103. The Rose and the Butterfly

A Butterfly once fell in love with a beautiful Rose. The Rose was not indifferent, for the Butterfly's wings were powdered in a charming pattern of gold and silver. And so, when he fluttered near and told how he loved her, she blushed rosily and said yes. After much pretty love-making and many whispered vows of constancy, the Butterfly took a tender leave of his sweetheart.

But alas! It was a long time before he came back to her.

"Is this your constancy?" she exclaimed tearfully. "It is ages since you went away, and all the time, you have been carrying on with all sorts of flowers. I saw you kiss Miss Geranium, and you fluttered around Miss

Mignonette until Honey Bee chased you away. I wish he had stung you!"

"Constancy!" laughed the Butterfly. "I had no sooner left you than I saw Zephyr kissing you. You carried on scandalously with Mr. Bumble Bee and you made eyes at every single Bug you could see. You can't expect any constancy from me!"

Do not expect constancy in others if you have none yourself.

104. The Cat and the Fox

Once a Cat and a Fox were traveling together. As they went along, picking up provisions on the way—a stray mouse here, a fat chicken there—they began an argument to while away the time between bites. And, as usually happens when comrades argue, the talk began to get personal.

"You think you are extremely clever, don't you?" said the Fox. "Do you pretend to know more than I? Why, I know a whole sackful of tricks!"

"Well," retorted the Cat, "I admit I know one trick only, but that one, let me tell you, is worth a thousand of yours!"

Just then, close by, they heard a hunter's horn and the yelping of a pack of hounds.

In an instant the Cat was up a tree, hiding among the leaves.

"This is my trick," he called to the Fox. "Now let me see what yours are worth."

But the Fox had so many plans for escape he could not decide which one to try first. He dodged here and there with the hounds at his heels. He doubled on his tracks, he ran at top speed, he entered a dozen burrows,—but all in vain. The hounds caught him, and soon put an end to the boaster and all his tricks.

Common sense is always worth more than cunning.

105. The Boy and the Nettle

A Boy, stung by a Nettle, ran home crying, to get his mother to blow on the hurt and kiss it.

"Son," said the Boy's mother, when she had comforted him, "the next time you come near a Nettle, grasp it firmly, and it will be as soft as silk."

Whatever you do, do with all your might.

106. The Old Lion

A Lion had grown very old. His teeth were worn away. His limbs could no longer bear him, and the King of Beasts was very pitiful indeed as he lay gasping on the ground, about to die. Where now his strength and his former graceful beauty?

Now a Boar spied him, and rushing at him, gored him with his yellow tusk. A Bull trampled him with his heavy hoofs. Even a contemptible Ass let fly his heels and brayed his insults in the face of the Lion.

It is cowardly to attack the defenseless, though he be an enemy.

107. The Fox and the Lion

A very young Fox, who had never before seen a Lion, happened to meet one in the forest. A single look was enough to send the Fox off at top speed for the nearest hiding place.

The second time the Fox saw the Lion he stopped behind a tree to look at him a

moment before slinking away. But the third time, the Fox went boldly up to the Lion and, without turning a hair, said,

"Hello, there, old top."

Familiarity breeds contempt.
Acquaintance with evil blinds us to its dangers.

108. The Fox and the Pheasants

One moonlight evening as Master Fox was taking his usual stroll in the woods, he saw a number of Pheasants perched quite out of his reach on a limb of a tall old tree. The sly Fox soon found a bright patch of moonlight, where the Pheasants could see him clearly; there he raised himself up on his hind legs, and began a wild dance. First he whirled 'round and 'round like a top, then he hopped up and down, cutting all sorts of strange capers. The Pheasants stared giddily. They hardly dared blink for fear of losing him out of their sight a single instant.

Now the Fox made as if to climb a tree, now he fell over and lay still, playing dead, and the next instant he was hopping on all fours, his back in the air, and his bushy tail shaking so that it seemed to throw out silver sparks in the moonlight. By this time the poor birds' heads were in a whirl. And when the Fox began his performance all over again, so dazed did they become, that they lost their hold on the limb, and fell down one by one to the Fox.

Too much attention to danger may cause us to fall victims to it.

109. Two Travelers and a Bear

Two Men were traveling in company through a forest, when, all at once, a huge Bear crashed out of the brush near them. One of the Men, thinking of his own safety, climbed a tree. The other, unable to fight the savage beast alone, threw himself on the ground and lay still, as if he were dead. He had heard that a Bear will not touch a dead body. It must have been true, for the Bear snuffed at the Man's head awhile, and then, seeming to be satisfied that he was dead, walked away.

The Man in the tree climbed down.

"It looked just as if that Bear whispered in your ear," he said. "What did he tell you?"

"He said," answered the other, "that it

was not at all wise to keep company with a fellow who would desert his friend in a moment of danger."

Misfortune is the test of true friendship.

110. The Porcupine and the Snakes

A Porcupine was looking for a good home. At last he found a little sheltered cave, where lived a family of Snakes. He asked them to let him share the cave with them, and the Snakes kindly consented.

The Snakes soon wished they had not given him permission to stay. His sharp quills pricked them at every turn, and at last they politely asked him to leave.

"I am very well satisfied, thank you," said the Porcupine. "I intend to stay right here." And with that, he politely escorted the Snakes out of doors. And to save their skins, the Snakes had to look for another home.

Give a finger and lose a hand.

111. The Fox and the Monkey

At a great meeting of the Animals, who had gathered to elect a new ruler, the Monkey was asked to dance. This he did so well, with a thousand funny capers and grimaces, that the Animals were carried entirely off their feet with enthusiasm, and then and there, elected him their king.

The Fox did not vote for the Monkey and was much disgusted with the Animals for electing so unworthy a ruler.

One day he found a trap with a bit of meat in it. Hurrying to King Monkey, he told him he had found a rich treasure, which he had not touched because it belonged by right to his majesty the Monkey.

The greedy Monkey followed the Fox

to the trap. As soon as he saw the meat he grasped eagerly for it, only to find himself held fast in the trap. The Fox stood off and laughed.

"You pretend to be our king," he said, "and cannot even take care of yourself!"

Shortly after that, another election among the Animals was held.

The true leader proves himself by his qualities.

112. The Mother and the Wolf

Early one morning a hungry Wolf was prowling around a cottage at the edge of a village, when he heard a child crying in the house. Then he heard the Mother's voice say:

"Hush, child, hush! Stop your crying, or I will give you to the Wolf!"

Surprised but delighted at the prospect of so delicious a meal, the Wolf settled down under an open window, expecting every moment to have the child handed out to him. But though the little one continued to fret, the Wolf waited all day in vain.

Then, toward nightfall, he heard the Mother's voice again as she sat down near the window to sing and rock her baby to sleep.

"There, child, there! The Wolf shall not get you. No, no! Daddy is watching and Daddy will kill him if he should come near!"

Just then the Father came within sight of the home, and the Wolf was barely able to save himself from the Dogs by a clever bit of running.

Do not believe everything you hear.

113. The Flies and the Honey

A jar of honey was upset and the sticky sweetness flowed out on the table. The sweet smell of the honey soon brought a large number of Flies buzzing around. They did not wait for an invitation. No, indeed; they settled right down, feet and all, to gorge themselves.

The Flies were quickly smeared from head to foot with honey. Their wings stuck together. They could not pull their feet out of the sticky mass. And so they died, giving their lives for the sake of a taste of sweetness.

Be not greedy for a little passing pleasure. It may destroy you.

114. The Fox and the Crow

One bright morning as the Fox was following his sharp nose through the wood in search of a bite to eat, he saw a Crow on the limb of a tree overhead. This was by no means the first Crow the Fox had ever seen. What caught his attention this time and made him stop for a second look, was that the lucky Crow held a bit of cheese in her beak.

'No need to search any farther,' thought sly Master Fox. 'Here is a dainty bite for my breakfast.'

Up he trotted to the foot of the tree in which the Crow was sitting, and looking up admiringly, he cried, "Good-morning, beautiful creature!"

The Crow, her head cocked on one side,

watched the Fox suspiciously. But she kept her beak tightly closed on the cheese and did not return his greeting.

"What a charming creature she is!" said the Fox. "How her feathers shine! What a beautiful form and what splendid wings! Such a wonderful Bird should have a very lovely voice, since everything else about her is so perfect. Could she sing just one song, I know I should hail her Queen of Birds."

Listening to these flattering words, the Crow forgot all her suspicion, and also her breakfast. She wanted very much to be called Queen of Birds. So she opened her beak wide to utter her loudest caw, and down fell the cheese straight into the Fox's open mouth.

"Thank you," said Master Fox sweetly, as he walked off. "Though it is cracked, you have a voice sure enough. But where are your wits?"

The flatterer lives at the expense of those who will listen to him.

115. The Eagle and the Kite

An Eagle sat high in the branches of a great Oak. She seemed very sad and drooping for an Eagle. A Kite saw her.

"Why do you look so woebegone?" asked the Kite.

"I want to get married," replied the Eagle, "and I can't find a mate who can provide for me as I should like."

"Take me," said the Kite; "I am very strong, stronger even than you!"

"Do you really think you can provide for me?" asked the Eagle eagerly. "Why, of course," replied the Kite. "That would be a very simple matter. I am so strong I can carry away an Ostrich in my talons as if it were a feather!"

The Eagle accepted the Kite immediately. But after the wedding, when the Kite flew away to find something to eat for his bride, all he had when he returned, was a tiny Mouse.

"Is that the Ostrich you talked about?" said the Eagle in disgust.

"To win you I would have said and promised anything," replied the Kite.

Everything is fair in love.

116. The Fir-Tree and the Bramble

A Fir-tree was boasting to a Bramble, and said, somewhat contemptuously, "You poor creature, you are of no use whatever. Now, look at me: I am useful for all sorts of things, particularly when men build houses; they can't do without me then."

But the Bramble replied, "Ah, that's all very well: but you wait till they come with axes and saws to cut you down, and then you'll wish you were a Bramble and not a Fir."

Better poverty without a care than wealth with its many obligations.

117. The Animals and the Plague

Once upon a time a severe plague raged among the animals. Many died, and those who lived were so ill, that they cared for neither food nor drink, and dragged themselves about listlessly. No longer could a fat young hen tempt Master Fox to dinner, nor a tender lamb rouse greedy Sir Wolf's appetite. At last the Lion decided to call a council. When all the animals were gathered together he arose and said:

"Dear friends, I believe the gods have sent this plague upon us as a punishment for our sins. Therefore, the most guilty one of us must be offered in sacrifice. Perhaps we may thus obtain forgiveness and cure for all.

"I will confess all my sins first. I admit

that I have been very greedy and have devoured many sheep. They had done me no harm. I have eaten goats and bulls and stags. To tell the truth, I even ate up a shepherd now and then.

"Now, if I am the most guilty, I am ready to be sacrificed. But I think it best that each one confess his sins as I have done. Then we can decide in all justice who is the most guilty."

"Your majesty," said the Fox, "you are too good. Can it be a crime to eat sheep, such stupid mutton heads? No, no, your majesty. You have done them great honor by eating them up.

"And so far as shepherds are concerned, we all know they belong to that puny race that pretends to be our masters."

All the animals applauded the Fox loudly. Then, though the Tiger, the Bear, the Wolf, and all the savage beasts recited the most wicked deeds, all were excused and made to appear very saint-like and innocent. It was now the Ass's turn to confess.

"I remember," he said guiltily, "that one day as I was passing a field belonging to some priests, I was so tempted by the tender grass and my hunger, that I could not resist nibbling a bit of it. I had no right to do it, I admit—"

A great uproar among the beasts interrupted him. Here was the culprit who had brought misfortune on all of them! What a horrible crime it was to eat grass that belonged to someone else! It was enough to hang anyone for, much more an Ass. Immediately they all fell upon him, the Wolf in the lead, and soon had made an end to him, sacrificing him to the gods then and there, and without the formality of an altar.

The weak are made to suffer for the misdeeds of the powerful.

118. The Shepherd and the Lion

A Shepherd, counting his Sheep one day, discovered that a number of them were missing. Much irritated, he very loudly and boastfully declared that he would catch the thief and punish him as he deserved. The Shepherd suspected a Wolf of the deed and so set out toward a rocky region among the hills, where there were caves infested by Wolves. But before starting out he made a vow to Jupiter that if he would help him find the thief he would offer a fat Calf as a sacrifice.

The Shepherd searched a long time without finding any Wolves, but just as he was passing near a large cave on the mountain side, a huge Lion stalked out, carrying a Sheep. In great terror the Shepherd fell on his knees.

"Alas, O Jupiter, man does not know what he asks! To find the thief I offered to sacrifice a fat Calf. Now I promise you a full-grown Bull, if you but make the thief go away!"

We are often not so eager for what we seek,
after we have found it.
Do not foolishly ask for things that would
bring ruin
if they were granted.

119. The Hare and the Tortoise

A Hare was making fun of the Tortoise one day for being so slow.

"Do you ever get anywhere?" he asked with a mocking laugh.

"Yes," replied the Tortoise, "and I get there sooner than you think. I'll run you a race and prove it."

The Hare was much amused at the idea of running a race with the Tortoise, but for the fun of the thing he agreed. So the Fox, who had consented to act as judge, marked the distance and started the runners off.

The Hare was soon far out of sight, and to make the Tortoise feel very deeply how ridiculous it was for him to try a race with a Hare, he lay down beside the course to take a nap until the Tortoise should catch up.

The Tortoise meanwhile kept going slowly but steadily, and, after a time, passed the place where the Hare was sleeping. But the Hare slept on very peacefully; and when at last he did wake up, the Tortoise was near the goal. The Hare now ran his swiftest, but he could not overtake the Tortoise in time.

The race is not always to the swift.

120. The Miller, His Son, and the Ass

One day, a long time ago, an old Miller and his Son were on their way to market with an Ass which they hoped to sell. They drove him very slowly, for they thought they would have a better chance to sell him if they kept him in good condition. As they walked along the highway some travelers laughed loudly at them.

"What foolishness," cried one, "to walk when they might as well ride. The most stupid of the three is not the one you would expect it to be."

The Miller did not like to be laughed at, so he told his son to climb up and ride. They had gone a little farther along the road, when three merchants passed by.

"Oho, what have we here?" they cried. "Respect old age, young man! Get down, and let the old man ride."

Though the Miller was not tired, he made the boy get down and climbed up him-

lf to ride, just to please the Merchants.

At the next turnstile they overtook some women carrying market baskets loaded with vegetables and other things to sell.

"Look at the old fool," exclaimed one of them. "Perched on the Ass, while that poor boy has to walk."

The Miller felt a bit vexed, but to be

agreeable he told the Boy to climb up behind him.

They had no sooner started out again than a loud shout went up from another company of people on the road.

"What a crime," cried one, "to load up a poor dumb beast like that! They look more able to carry the poor creature, than he to carry them."

"They must be on their way to sell the poor thing's hide," said another.

The Miller and his Son quickly scrambled down, and a short time later, the market place was thrown into an uproar as the two came along carrying the Donkey slung from a pole. A great crowd of people ran out to get a closer look at the strange sight.

The Ass did not dislike being carried,

but so many people came up to point at him and laugh and shout, that he began to kick and bray, and then, just as they were crossing a bridge, the ropes that held him gave way, and down he tumbled into the river.

The poor Miller now set out sadly for home. By trying to please everybody, he had pleased nobody, and lost his Ass besides.

If you try to please all, you please none.

121. The Bees, the Wasps, and the Hornet

A store of honey had been found in a hollow tree, and the Wasps declared positively that it belonged to them. The Bees were just as sure that the treasure was theirs.

The argument grew very pointed, and it looked as if the affair could not be settled without a battle, when at last, with much good sense, they agreed to let a judge decide the matter. So they brought the case before the Hornet, justice of the peace in that part of the woods.

When the Judge called the case, witnesses declared that they had seen certain winged creatures in the neighborhood of the hollow tree, who hummed loudly, and whose bodies were striped, yellow and black, like Bees.

Counsel for the Wasps immediately insisted that this description fitted his clients exactly. Such evidence did not help Judge Hornet to any decision, so he adjourned court for six weeks to give him time to think it over.

When the case came up again, both sides had a large number of witnesses. An Ant was first to take the stand, and was about to be cross-examined, when a wise old Bee addressed the Court.

"Your honor," he said, "the case has now been pending for six weeks. If it is not decided soon, the honey will not be fit for anything. I move that the Bees and the Wasps be both instructed to build a honey comb. Then we shall soon see to whom the honey really belongs."

The Wasps protested loudly. Wise Judge Hornet quickly understood why they did so: They knew they could not build a honey comb and fill it with honey.

"It is clear," said the Judge, "who made the comb and who could not have made it. The honey belongs to the Bees."

Ability proves itself by deeds.

122. The Lark and Her Young Ones

A Lark made her nest in a field of young wheat. As the days passed, the wheat stalks grew tall and the young birds, too, grew in strength. Then one day, when the ripe golden grain waved in the breeze, the Farmer and his son came into the field.

"This wheat is now ready for reaping," said the Farmer. "We must call in our neighbors and friends to help us harvest it."

The young Larks in their nest close by were much frightened, for they knew they would be in great danger if they did not leave the nest before the reapers came. When the Mother Lark returned with food for them, they told her what they had heard.

"Do not be frightened, children," said

the Mother Lark. "If the Farmer said he would call in his neighbors and friends to help him do his work, this wheat will not be reaped for a while yet."

A few days later, the wheat was so ripe, that when the wind shook the stalks, a hail of wheat grains came rustling down on the young Larks' heads.

"If this wheat is not harvested at once," said the Farmer, "we shall lose half the crop. We cannot wait any longer for help from our friends. Tomorrow we must set to work, ourselves."

When the young Larks told their mother what they had heard that day, she said:

"Then we must be off at once. When a man decides to do his own work and not depend on any one else, then you may be sure there will be no more delay."

There was much fluttering and trying out of wings that afternoon, and at sunrise next day, when the Farmer and his son cut down the grain, they found an empty nest.

Self-help is the best help.

123. The Cat and the Old Rat

There was once a Cat who was so watchful, that a Mouse hardly dared show the tip of his whiskers for fear of being eaten alive. That Cat seemed to be everywhere at once with his claws all ready for a pounce. At last the Mice kept so closely to their dens, that the Cat saw he would have to use his wits well to catch one.

So one day he climbed up on a shelf and hung from it, head downward, as if he were dead, holding himself up by clinging to some ropes with one paw. When the Mice peeped out and saw him in that position, they thought he had been hung up there in punishment for some misdeed. Very timidly at first they stuck out their heads and sniffed about carefully. But as nothing stirred, all trooped joyfully out to celebrate the death of the Cat. Just then the Cat let go his hold, and before the Mice recovered from their surprise, he had made an end of three or four.

Now the Mice kept more strictly at home than ever. But the Cat, who was still hungry for Mice, knew more tricks than one. Rolling himself in flour until he was covered completely, he lay down in the flour bin, with one eye open for the Mice. Sure enough, the Mice soon began to come out. To the Cat it was almost as if he already had a plump young Mouse under his claws, when an old Rat, who had had much experience with Cats and traps, and had even lost a part of his tail to pay for it, sat up at a safe distance from a hole in the wall where he lived.

"Take care!" he cried. "That may be a heap of meal, but it looks to me very much like the Cat. Whatever it is, it is wisest to keep at a safe distance.”

The wise do not let themselves be tricked a second time.

124. The Ass and It's Shadow

A Traveler had hired an Ass to carry him to a distant part of the country. The owner of the Ass went with the Traveler, walking beside him to drive the Ass and point out the way.

The road led across a treeless plain where the Sun beat down fiercely. So intense did the heat become, that the Traveler at last decided to stop for a rest, and as there was no other shade to be found, the Traveler sat down in the shadow of the Ass.

Now the heat had affected the Driver as much as it had the Traveler, and even more, for he had been walking. Wishing also to rest in the shade cast by the Ass, he began to quarrel with the Traveler, saying he had hired the Ass and not the shadow it cast.

The two soon came to blows, and while they were fighting, the Ass took to its heels.

In quarreling about the shadow we often lose the substance.

125. The Ant and the Dove

A Dove saw an Ant fall into a brook. The Ant struggled in vain to reach the bank, and in pity, the Dove dropped a blade of straw close beside it. Clinging to the straw like a shipwrecked sailor to a broken spar, the Ant floated safely to shore.

Soon after, the Ant saw a man getting ready to kill the Dove with a stone. But just as he cast the stone, the Ant stung him in the heel, so that the pain made him miss his aim, and the startled Dove flew to safety in a distant wood.

A kindness is never wasted.

126. The Man and the Satyr

A long time ago a Man met a Satyr in the forest and succeeded in making friends with him. The two soon became the best of comrades, living together in the Man's hut.

But one cold winter evening, as they were walking homeward, the Satyr saw the

Man blow on his fingers.

"Why do you do that?" asked the Satyr.

"To warm my hands," the Man replied.

When they reached home the Man prepared two bowls of porridge. These he placed steaming hot on the table, and the comrades sat down very cheerfully to enjoy the meal. But much to the Satyr's surprise, the Man began to blow into his bowl of por-

ridge.

"Why do you do that?" he asked.

"To cool my porridge," replied the Man.

The Satyr sprang hurriedly to his feet and made for the door.

"Goodby," he said, "I've seen enough. A fellow that blows hot and cold in the same breath cannot be friends with me!"

The man who talks for both sides is not to be trusted by either.

127. The Wolf, the Kid, and the Goat

Mother Goat was going to market one morning to get provisions for her household, which consisted of but one little Kid and herself.

"Take good care of the house, my son," she said to the Kid, as she carefully latched the door. "Do not let anyone in, unless he gives you this password: 'Down with the Wolf and all his race!'"

Strangely enough, a Wolf was lurking near and heard what the Goat had said. So, as soon as Mother Goat was out of sight, up he trotted to the door and knocked. "Down with the Wolf and all his race," said the Wolf softly. It was the right password, but when the Kid peeped through a crack in the door and saw the shadowy figure outside, he did not feel at all easy.

"Show me a white paw," he said, "or I won't let you in."

A white paw, of course, is a feature few Wolves can show, and so Master Wolf had to go away as hungry as he had come.

"You can never be too sure," said the Kid, when he saw the Wolf making off to the woods.

Two sureties are better than one.

128. The Swallow and the Crow

The Swallow and the Crow had an argument one day about their plumage.

Said the Swallow: "Just look at my bright and downy feathers. Your black stiff quills are not worth having. Why don't you dress better? Show a little pride!"

"Your feathers may do very well in spring," replied the Crow, "but—I don't remember ever having seen you around in winter, and that's when I enjoy myself most."

Friends in fine weather only, are not worth much.

129. Jupiter and the Monkey

There was once a baby show among the Animals in the forest. Jupiter provided the prize. Of course all the proud mammas from far and near brought their babies.

But none got there earlier than Mother Monkey. Proudly she presented her baby among the other contestants. As you can imagine, there was quite a laugh when the Animals saw the ugly flat-nosed, hairless, pop-eyed little creature.

"Laugh if you will," said the Mother Monkey. "Though Jupiter may not give him the prize, I know that he is the prettiest, the sweetest, the dearest darling in the world."

Mother love is blind.

130. The Lion's Share

A long time ago, the Lion, the Fox, the Jackal, and the Wolf agreed to go hunting together, sharing with each other whatever they found.One day the Wolf ran down a Stag and immediately called his comrades to divide the spoil. Without being asked, the Lion placed himself at the head of the feast to do the carving, and, with a great show of fairness, began to count the guests.

"One," he said, counting on his claws, "that is myself the Lion. Two, that's the Wolf, three, is the Jackal, and the Fox makes four."

He then very carefully divided the Stag into four equal parts.

"I am King Lion," he said, when he had

finished, "so of course I get the first part. This next part falls to me because I am the strongest; and this is mine because I am the bravest."

He now began to glare at the others very savagely. "If any of you have any claim to the part that is left," he growled, stretching his claws meaningly, "now is the time to speak up."

Might makes right.

131. The Lion, the Ass, and the Fox

A Lion, an Ass, and a Fox were hunting in company, and caught a large quantity of game. The Ass was asked to divide the spoil. This he did very fairly, giving each an equal share. The Fox was well satisfied, but the Lion flew into a great rage over it, and with

one stroke of his huge paw, he added the Ass to the pile of slain. Then he turned to the Fox.

"You divide it," he roared angrily.

The Fox wasted no time in talking. He quickly piled all the game into one great heap. From this he took a very small portion for himself, such undesirable bits as the horns and hoofs of a mountain goat, and the end of an ox tail.

The Lion now recovered his good humor entirely.

"Who taught you to divide so fairly?" he asked pleasantly.

"I learned a lesson from the Ass," replied the Fox, carefully edging away.

Learn from the misfortunes of others.

132. The Mole and His Mother

A little Mole once said to his Mother:

"Why, Mother, you said I was blind! But I am sure I can see!"

Mother Mole saw she would have to get such conceit out of his head. So she put a bit of frankincense before him and asked him to tell what it was.

The little Mole peered at it.

"Why, that's a pebble!"

"Well, my son, that proves you've lost your sense of smell as well as being blind."

Boast of one thing and you will be found lacking in that
and a few other things as well.

133. The Hare and His Ears

The Lion had been badly hurt by the horns of a Goat, which he was eating. He was very angry to think that any animal that he chose for a meal, should be so brazen as to wear such dangerous things as horns to scratch him while he ate.

So he commanded that all animals with horns should leave his domains within twenty-four hours. The command struck terror among the beasts. All those who were so unfortunate as to have horns, began to pack up and move out. Even the Hare, who, as you know, has no horns and so had nothing to fear, passed a very restless night, dreaming awful dreams about the fearful Lion. And when he came out of the warren in the early morning sunshine, and there saw the shadow cast by his long and pointed ears, a terrible fright seized him.

"Goodby, neighbor Cricket," he called. "I'm off. He will certainly make out that my ears are horns, no matter what I say."

Do not give your enemies the slightest reason to attack your reputation.

Your enemies will seize any excuse to attack you.

134. The Wolves and the Sheep

A pack of Wolves lurked near the Sheep pasture. But the Dogs kept them all at a respectful distance, and the Sheep grazed in perfect safety. But now the Wolves thought of a plan to trick the Sheep.

"Why is there always this hostility between us?" they said. "If it were not for those Dogs who are always stirring up trouble, I am sure we should get along beautifully. Send them away and you will see what good friends we shall become."

The Sheep were easily fooled. They persuaded the Dogs to go away, and that very evening the Wolves had the grandest feast of their lives.

Do not give up friends for foes.

135. The North Wind and the Sun

The North Wind and the Sun had a quarrel about which of them was the stronger. While they were disputing with much heat and bluster, a Traveler passed along the road wrapped in a cloak.

"Let us agree," said the Sun, "that he is the stronger who can strip that Traveler of his cloak."

"Very well," growled the North Wind, and at once sent a cold, howling blast against the Traveler.

With the first gust of wind the ends of the cloak whipped about the Traveler's body.

But he immediately wrapped it closely around him, and the harder the Wind blew, the tighter he held it to him. The North Wind

tore angrily at the cloak, but all his efforts were in vain.

Then the Sun began to shine. At first his beams were gentle, and in the pleasant warmth after the bitter cold of the North Wind, the Traveler unfastened his cloak and let it hang loosely from his shoulders.

The Sun's rays grew warmer and warmer. The man took off his cap and mopped his brow. At last he became so heated that he pulled off his cloak, and, to escape the blazing sunshine, threw himself down in the welcome shade of a tree by the roadside.

Gentleness and kind persuasion win where force and bluster fail.

136. The Blacksmith and His Dog

A Blacksmith had a little Dog, which used to sleep when his master was at work, but was very wide awake indeed when it was time for meals.

One day his master pretended to be disgusted at this, and when he had thrown him a bone as usual, he said, "What on earth is the good of a lazy cur like you? When I am hammering away at my anvil, you just curl up and go to sleep: but no sooner do I stop for a mouthful of food than you wake up and wag your tail to be fed."

Those who will not work deserve to starve.

137. The Fisherman and the Little Fish

A poor Fisherman, who lived on the fish he caught, had bad luck one day and caught nothing but a very small fry. The Fisherman was about to put it in his basket when the little Fish said:

"Please spare me, Mr. Fisherman! I am so small it is not worth while to carry me home. When I am bigger, I shall make you a much better meal."

But the Fisherman quickly put the fish into his basket.

"How foolish I should be," he said, "to throw you back. However small you may be, you are better than nothing at all."

A small gain is worth more than a large promise.

138. The Fighting Cocks and the Eagle

Once there were two Cocks living in the same farmyard who could not bear the sight of each other. At last one day they flew up to fight it out, beak and claw. They fought until one of them was beaten and crawled off to a corner to hide. The Cock that had won the battle flew to the top of the hen-house, and, proudly flapping his wings, crowed with all his might to tell the world about his victory.

But an Eagle, circling overhead, heard the boasting chanticleer and, swooping down, carried him off to his nest. His rival saw the deed, and coming out of his corner, took his place as master of the farmyard.

Pride goes before a fall.

139. The Bee and Jupiter

A Queen Bee from Hymettus flew up to Olympus with some fresh honey from the hive as a present to Jupiter, who was so pleased with the gift that he promised to give her anything she liked to ask for. She said she would be very grateful if he would give stings to the bees, to kill people who robbed them of their honey.

Jupiter was greatly displeased with this request, for he loved mankind: but he had given his word, so he said that stings they should have. The stings he gave them, however, were of such a kind that whenever a bee stings a man the sting is left in the wound and the bee dies.

Evil wishes, like fowls, come home to roost.

140. The Blind Man and the Cub

There was once a Blind Man who had so fine a sense of touch that, when any animal was put into his hands, he could tell what it was merely by the feel of it.

One day the Cub of a Wolf was put into his hands, and he was asked what it was. He felt it for some time, and then said, "Indeed, I am not sure whether it is a Wolf's Cub or a Fox's: but this I know—it would never do to trust it in a sheepfold."

Evil tendencies are early shown.

141. The Dog and the Cook

A rich man once invited a number of his friends and acquaintances to a banquet. His dog thought it would be a good opportunity to invite another Dog, a friend of his; so he went to him and said, "My master is giving a feast: there'll be a fine spread, so come and dine with me to-night."

The Dog thus invited came, and when he saw the preparations being made in the kitchen he said to himself, "My word, I'm in luck: I'll take care to eat enough to-night to last me two or three days."

At the same time he wagged his tail briskly, by way of showing his friend how delighted he was to have been asked.

But just then the Cook caught sight

of him, and, in his annoyance at seeing a strange Dog in the kitchen, caught him up by the hind legs and threw him out of the window.

He had a nasty fall, and limped away as quickly as he could, howling dismally.

Presently some other dogs met him, and said, "Well, what sort of a dinner did you get?" To which he replied, "I had a splendid time: the wine was so good, and I drank so much of it, that I really don't remember how I got out of the house!"

Be shy of favours bestowed at the expense of others.

142. The Boy Bathing

A Boy was bathing in a river and got out of his depth, and was in great danger of being drowned. A man who was passing along a road heard his cries for help, and went to the riverside and began to scold him for being so careless as to get into deep water, but

made no attempt to help him.

"Oh, sir," cried the Boy, "please help me first and scold me afterwards."

Give assistance, not advice, in a crisis.

143. The Peasant and the Apple Tree

A Peasant had an Apple Tree growing in his garden, which bore no fruit, but merely served to provide a shelter from the heat for the sparrows and grasshoppers which sat and chirped in its branches. Disappointed at its barrenness he determined to cut it down, and went and fetched his axe for the purpose. But when the sparrows and the grasshoppers saw what he was about to do, they begged him to spare it, and said to him, "If you destroy the tree we shall have to seek shelter elsewhere, and you will no longer have our merry chirping to enliven your work in the garden."

He, however, refused to listen to them, and set to work with a will to cut through the trunk. A few strokes showed that it was hollow inside and contained a swarm of bees and a large store of honey. Delighted with his find he threw down his axe, saying, "The old tree is worth keeping after all."

Utility is most men's test of worth.

144. The Farmer and the Fox

A Farmer was greatly annoyed by a Fox, which came prowling about his yard at night and carried off his fowls. So he set a trap for him and caught him; and in order to be revenged upon him, he tied a bunch of tow to his tail and set fire to it and let him go.

As ill-luck would have it, however, the Fox made straight for the fields where the corn was standing ripe and ready for cutting. It quickly caught fire and was all burnt up, and the Farmer lost all his harvest.

Revenge is a two-edged sword.

145. The Cage-Bird and the Bat

A Singing-bird was confined in a cage which hung outside a window, and had a way of singing at night when all other birds were asleep.

One night a Bat came and clung to the bars of the cage, and asked the Bird why she was silent by day and sang only at night. "I have a very good reason for doing so," said the Bird: "it was once when I was singing in the daytime that a fowler was attracted by my voice, and set his nets for me and caught me. Since then I have never sung except by night."

But the Bat replied, "It is no use your doing that now when you are a prisoner: if only you had done so before you were caught, you might still have been free."

Precautions are useless after the event.

146. The Ass and His Masters

A Gardener had an Ass which had a very hard time of it, what with scanty food, heavy loads, and constant beating. The Ass therefore begged Jupiter to take him away from the Gardener and hand him over to another master. So Jupiter sent Mercury to the Gardener to bid him sell the Ass to a Potter, which he did.

But the Ass was as discontented as ever, for he had to work harder than before: so he begged Jupiter for relief a second time, and Jupiter very obligingly arranged that he should be sold to a Tanner. But when the Ass saw what his new master's trade was, he cried in despair, "Why wasn't I content to serve either of my former masters, hard as I had to work and badly as I was treated? for they would have buried me decently, but now I shall come in the end to the tanning-vat."

Servants don't know a good master
till they have served a worse.

147. The Frogs and the Well

Two Frogs lived together in a marsh. But one hot summer the marsh dried up, and they left it to look for another place to live in: for frogs like damp places if they can get them. By and by they came to a deep well, and one of them looked down into it, and said to the other, "This looks a nice cool place: let us jump in and settle here."

But the other, who had a wiser head on his shoulders, replied, "Not so fast, my friend: supposing this well dried up like the marsh, how should we get out again?"

Think twice before you act.

148. The Bee-Keeper

A Thief found his way into an apiary when the Bee-keeper was away, and stole all the honey. When the Keeper returned and found the hives empty, he was very much upset and stood staring at them for some time.

Before long the bees came back from gathering honey, and, finding their hives overturned and the Keeper standing by, they made for him with their stings. At this he fell into a passion and cried, "You ungrateful scoundrels, you let the thief who stole my honey get off scot-free, and then you go and sting me who have always taken such care of you!"

When you hit back make sure you have got the right man.

149. The Impostor

A certain man fell ill, and, being in a very bad way, he made a vow that he would sacrifice a hundred oxen to the gods if they would grant him a return to health. Wishing to see how he would keep his vow, they caused him to recover in a short time. Now, he hadn't an ox in the world, so he made a hundred little oxen out of tallow and offered them up on an altar, at the same time saying, "Ye gods, I call you to witness that I have discharged my vow."

The gods determined to be even with him, so they sent him a dream, in which he was bidden to go to the sea-shore and fetch a hundred crowns which he was to find there. Hastening in great excitement to the shore, he fell in with a band of robbers, who seized him and carried him off to sell as a slave: and when they sold him a hundred crowns was the sum he fetched.

Do not promise more than you can perform.

150. The Nightingale and the Swallow

A Swallow, conversing with a Nightingale, advised her to quit the leafy coverts where she made her home, and to come and live with men, like herself, and nest under the shelter of their roofs. But the Nightingale replied, "Time was when I too, like yourself, lived among men: but the memory of the cruel wrongs I then suffered makes them hateful to me, and never again will I approach their dwellings."

The scene of past sufferings revives painful memories.

memo

memo

memo

memo

memo

memo

THE CLASSIC
An Imprint of MIRBOOK COMPANY Publishing Co,.
2F, 12 Seongmisan-ro 32-gil, Mapo-gu, Seoul, South Korea
T; +82 2 3141 4421 | F; +82 2 3141 4428
E-mail; sanhonjinju@naver.com

Aesop's Fables 1
By Aesop | Arthur Rackham

Published by MIRBOOK COMPANY Co,.